Robin Hood
Baking
Festival
COOKBOOK

Robin Hood

Baking Festival
COOKBOOK

Robert
ROSE

Disclaimer
The recipes in this book have been carefully tested by our kitchen and our tasters. To the best of
our knowledge, they are safe and nutritious for ordinary use and users. For those people with
food or other allergies, or who have special food requirements or health issues, please read the
suggested contents of each recipe carefully and determine whether or not they may create a
problem for you. All recipes are used at the risk of the consumer.

We cannot be responsible for any hazards, loss or damage which may occur as a result of any
recipe use.

For those with special needs, allergies, requirements or health problems, in the event of any
doubt, please contact your medical adviser prior to the use of any recipe.

National Library of Canada Cataloguing in Publication Data

Main entry under title:
   Robin Hood baking festival cookbook

Includes index.
Recipes compiled from Robin Hood's annual baking festival.
ISBN 0-7788-0040-7

1. Baking I. Robin Hood Multifoods Inc.

TX765.R628 2001   641.8'15   C2001-900967-4

Cover: Cherry Almond Coffee Cake (recipe, p. 72). *Photo page 1:* Chocolate Chunk
Pecan Cookies (recipe, p. 118). *Photo page 2:* Open Apple Plum Pie (recipe, p. 62).
Photo page 6: Lemon Sugar Wafers and Butterscotch No-Bakes (recipes, p. 122).

Design & Production: PageWave Graphics Inc.
Editor: Carol Sherman
Copy Editor: Julia Armstrong
Photography: Robert Wigington
Food Stylist: Jill Snider
Prop Stylist: Maggi Jones, Sue Florian
Color Scans & Film: Colour Technologies

We acknowledge the financial support of the Government of Canada through the
Book Publishing Industry Development Program (BPIDP) for our publishing activities.

Published by: Robert Rose Inc.
120 Eglinton Ave. E., Suite 1000, Toronto, Ontario, Canada M4P 1E2
Tel: (416) 322-6552 Fax: (416) 322-6936

Printed in Canada

1 2 3 4 5 6 7 8 9 10   F   09 08 07 06 05 04 03 02 01

Robin Hood

Robin Hood Multifoods is one of Canada's leading food companies, and its flour products are a household name across Canada. Robin Hood's first flour mill went into operation in Moose Jaw, Saskatchewan, in 1909. Since then, we have grown to be a market leader in the flour business, with mills in Montreal, Port Colborne and Saskatoon.

Much of our success has come from the long-term relationship we have developed with Canada's bakers. Generations of consumers have found Robin Hood flour to be of consistently high quality because we use only the very best Canadian wheat, which is then milled and packed to the highest and most exacting standards. Robin Hood flour will deliver excellent baking results every time.

In 1982, we introduced The Robin Hood Baking Festival to help Canadian bakers find interesting recipes to expand their snack and dessert menus. Over the years, thousands of recipes have been developed, modified, adjusted and triple tested, and hundreds of these recipes have been featured in our Baking Festival recipe booklets each fall.

With the *Robin Hood Baking Festival Cookbook* we are responding to thousands of consumer inquiries by reprinting more than 100 of our favorite recipes. We hope you enjoy making these recipes as much as we enjoyed sharing them.

Contents

Acknowledgements

I'd like to express sincere thanks to the many talented and devoted people who helped put this book together: the publisher, Bob Dees, who convinced us to compile our best Baking Festival recipes into one book for consumers to enjoy as they have since 1982, and who worked with us to make it a reality; Andrew Smith and Joseph Gisini, who designed and laid out the book; Brenda Venedam, who accurately input the recipes; and Carol Sherman and Julia Armstrong for their eagle eyes in editing.

At Robin Hood, thanks to Jim Coles and Danielle Szostak for their support and understanding of the demanding workload required to meet deadlines; the large number of employees who have critically tasted and evaluated every recipe until perfected; Michelle, Sarah and Dan of Consumer Services, who spent countless hours proofreading the recipes to ensure their accuracy and who pleasantly answer endless consumer calls; the marketing group with whom I work very closely to produce the booklet every year; the sales force, who diligently promote the book and set up wonderful in-store Baking Festival displays.

I also wish to thank Robert Wigington, the outstanding photographer I've worked with for the past 25 years, who always manages to make even the most difficult shots jump off the page, and Maggi Jones and Sue Florian, the creative prop stylists.

My deepest gratitude to the many partners who have participated in the book, giving consumers a wide variety of the superior recipes they've come to expect from Robin Hood.

— Jill Snider

Introduction

Whenever thoughts turn to hearth and home, they inevitably gravitate toward home baking. Nothing epitomizes domestic comfort more than freshly baked bread, warm pudding, or crisp, buttery cookies cooling on a wire rack. But more than that, baked goods are central to our everyday lives. From morning toast or muffin to coffee-break cake to a decadent dinner-party dessert, these ultimate comfort foods have woven themselves deeply into the fabric of daily life. And what would our grandest celebrations, such as birthdays or weddings, be without a showstopper cake? Plain or fancy, simple or rich, old-fashioned or elegant — almost everyone cherishes a memory linked with freshly baked goods. So, not surprisingly, creating these mouthwatering treats to share with family and friends can be one of life's great pleasures.

Whether you are a novice or experienced baker, the *Robin Hood Baking Festival Cookbook* will inspire you to explore the wonderful world of baking. Although the basic ingredients couldn't be simpler — flour combined with some combination of salt, eggs, sweetener, leavening agent or fat such as butter or shortening — the endless ways these ingredients can be varied make baking a great adventure. Fruits, nuts, grains, chocolate, dairy products and a wide range of flavorings can be mixed and matched with the essential components to create an array of delectable tastes, textures and sensations.

With more than a hundred easy-to-follow recipes and an abundance of luscious photographs, this book is destined to become an indispensable resource in kitchens from coast to coast. Intended for home cooks, the *Robin Hood Baking Festival Cookbook* is filled with dependable and delicious recipes that use basic ingredients. If they aren't already in your pantry, they will be readily available at your local grocery store. We hope these recipes will inspire you to create delicious baked goods that are uniquely yours.

Baking Basics

Although baking isn't difficult, it is a skill. Successful baking involves accurate measuring, proper techniques and careful attention to details such as oven temperature and cooking times. It also depends on following a well-tested recipe, understanding basic techniques and using the right equipment and ingredients. Read the following section on Baking Basics and learn how to avoid common pitfalls and achieve outstanding results every time you bake.

OVEN TEMPERATURE

Oven temperature plays a critical role in baking. Since ovens are often 25°F (10°C) hotter or cooler than their setting, we recommend that you become familiar with how your oven bakes. You can use a reliable oven thermometer to gauge the temperature in relation to the setting or you can gain a sense of whether your oven is hotter or cooler than the setting by carefully observing how quickly or slowly it cooks in relation to the recipes you use. Because oven temperatures vary so much, we recommend that you treat all recipe times as guidelines and routinely check what you are baking before the suggested times.

BAKING EQUIPMENT

Using the right equipment is an important part of successful baking. Good-quality, shiny metal pans and sheets are preferable because they bake evenly and do not rust. If you use glass pans, we suggest decreasing the oven temperature by 25°F (10°C). If using nonstick pans, follow the manufacturer's directions. Most recommend decreasing the temperature by 25°F (10°C) since nonstick surfaces, especially those that are dark, bake faster.

Using a pan other than the one called for or one made out of a material other than that specified in the recipe can dramatically affect results. Today's baking pans are not as standardized as they once were; they differ in size and shape from older ones and they also vary from one manufacturer to another. The labeling shows a mixture of imperial and metric measurements, which is often confusing.

To achieve optimum results, we recommend using the pan size specified in the recipe. However, you can substitute a pan that is similar in dimension and volume — just make sure you don't use a pan that is smaller in volume, as there may not be enough room to accommodate the expansion that takes place during baking. You can also interchange shapes (e.g. round instead of square) if the volume is the same and the pan is not much deeper, shallower, longer or shorter. Measurements are taken on the inside across the top of the pan. To confirm the volume of a pan, fill it with water, then pour the liquid into a measuring cup.

EQUIPMENT FOR SUCCESSFUL BAKING

Pans: To prepare the recipes in this book, you will need the following pans:

- 9-inch (2.5 L) square cake pan
- 8-inch (2 L) square cake pan
- two or three 8-inch (1.2 L) round cake pans
- two or three 9-inch (1.5 L) round cake pans
- 10-inch (3 L) Bundt pan
- 10-inch (4 L) tube pan
- 10-inch (25 cm) springform pan
- 8½-inch (21 cm) or 9-inch (23 cm) springform pan
- two 8½- by 4½-inch (1.5 L) or 9- by 5-inch (2 L) loaf pans
- two muffin (cupcake) pans (12 cups each) or a 24-cup muffin pan
- 13- by 9-inch (3.5 L) cake pan
- 17- by 11-inch (3 L) jelly roll pan or baking sheet with sides
- 15- by 10-inch (2 L) jelly roll pan
- three cookie sheets without sides
- 9-inch (23 cm) pie plate, preferably deep dish
- 9-inch (23 cm) flan pan with removable sides

Racks: Wire racks are essential for cooling cakes and cookies. Look for racks that have narrow spaces between the steel wires. It's a good idea to have a variety of sizes (round, square, rectangular) to suit whatever you're making. We recommend stainless steel racks since they won't rust and have a long life.

If you don't like rack marks on the top of your cake, keep one rack covered with a thick tea towel pinned securely in place. When necessary, remove the towel for washing.

Bowls: Every kitchen needs a variety of bowls in different sizes for combining and mixing ingredients. Metal or glass bowls are preferable. Plastic does not work well for beating egg whites as it retains oils, which can affect results. Have a few bowls of each size: small, medium and large.

The bowl needed for an electric mixer is a "mixer bowl." If the recipe doesn't specify a mixer bowl, other bowls will do (for example, when mixing a crumble topping or fruit with sugar).

Measuring Cups and Spoons: You will need glass or clear plastic measuring cups for liquid ingredients, a set of graduated dry ingredient measures, and a set of measuring spoons. (See Measure Accurately, page 14.)

Wire Whisks: Even if you use an electric mixer, you should have one medium-size all-purpose whisk for aerating dry ingredients or beating eggs before they are added to batters. If you don't have an electric mixer, a large balloon whisk is essential for jobs such as whipping cream or beating egg whites.

Zester: Some recipes call for the grated zest of oranges, lemons or limes, which adds indispensable flavor to many desserts. This inexpensive gadget, with tiny teeth, easily grates off the flavorful skin, separating it from the bitter white pith.

Cookie Cutters: An assortment of cookie cutters in different designs and shapes is both useful and fun. For many round cookies and biscuits, an inverted glass dipped in flour works very well.

Rolling Pin: A rolling pin is essential for making pie crusts and certain kinds of cookies. There are many different rolling pins on the market. It's worth investing some time to find the one that works best for you. A pastry cloth and stockinet cover for the rolling pin make life easy when it comes to rolling out pastry and cookie dough. They are available in most stores where kitchen equipment is sold.

Spatulas: You should have two rubber spatulas for such tasks as folding ingredients and scraping down the sides of a mixing bowl. Metal spatulas are also required for lifting cakes and cookies from pans and racks and for applying frostings to cakes. A small metal spatula is handy for frosting cakes.

Pastry Brushes: Pastry brushes are useful for brushing pastry with a wash or a glaze, or for greasing pans.

Parchment Paper: This baking tool is available in large sheets and rolls or cut to fit round pans. It is heatproof and is used to line pans and cookie sheets, making them nonstick.

Knives: A sharp serrated knife with a blade about 12 inches (30 cm) long makes cutting cakes horizontally a breeze. However, some people prefer to use dental floss for an even slice. Try both methods and pick your favorite. Electric knives are excellent for cutting angel food cakes. A good-quality chef's knife is also essential for chopping ingredients.

Pastry Bags and Tips: Although rarely essential, these devices, which can be used to shape batters and icings, give home baking a professional look. If you are writing names or greetings in frosting, a plastic squeeze bottle makes an acceptable substitute.

Mixer: Use an electric countertop mixer or a good-quality hand mixer, not the heavy-duty commercial type, which is too powerful for normal consumer-style baking. If you do a lot of baking, the countertop model is much more efficient and easier to use.

Food Processor: A food processor is a valuable kitchen tool that performs many kitchen tasks. It is very useful for bakers as it quickly chops ingredients such as fruits and nuts and purées mixtures. It also prepares an excellent pie crust, quickly cutting the fat into tiny ingredients and distributing it evenly throughout the dough.

Microwave Oven: Although a microwave oven is not essential, it is useful for baking functions such as melting chocolate or softening cold butter before it is creamed.

Bread Machine: A bread machine is a great addition to any household as it allows you to make freshly baked bread on a regular basis. It is also ideal for mixing yeast doughs, which can then be attractively shaped and finished in a conventional oven.

Baking Tips and Techniques

BE PREPARED

The first step to baking success is reading the recipe carefully, from beginning to end, before you begin to bake. After you've read the recipe, assemble all the ingredients and equipment in clear view on the counter. Few things are more frustrating than not being able to locate an ingredient when you're in the midst of mixing. You don't want to leave something out or be madly searching for a pan when your cake should be in the oven.

Allow adequate time to soften butter and bring cold ingredients such as eggs to room temperature. At least 15 minutes before you plan to bake, preheat your oven, being aware that some brands of ovens take longer to reach the desired temperature.

Prepare pans and baking sheets, if required, by greasing lightly with shortening or a vegetable cooking spray. Don't use butter, margarine or oil; they are more likely to stick and burn. If the pan needs to be floured as well, sprinkle the flour lightly over the greased surface. Shake the pan to distribute the flour evenly, then shake out the excess. Pans and baking sheets can also be lined with parchment paper, which ensures foolproof removal.

MEASURE ACCURATELY

Inaccurate measuring is one of the most common mistakes in baking. Every kitchen needs a set of graduated measures specifically intended for dry ingredients. These have a straight rim so that the ingredient being measured can be leveled off. To measure dry ingredients, spoon them lightly into the cup (you want them to be reasonably airy). Don't tap or pack. Then, using a spatula or a knife, level off. Flour and granulated and confectioner's (icing) sugar should all be measured by this method, before sifting unless otherwise specified.

Brown sugar is measured differently from other dry ingredients. It is packed firmly into the measure, then leveled off. If you invert the measure and tap the bottom, brown sugar, when properly measured, should unmold in the shape of the cup.

Liquids should be measured in clear glass or plastic liquid measuring cups, and the measurement should be read at eye level.

To accurately measure solid fats such as butter, margarine or shortening, use the water displacement method. For example, if a recipe calls for $\frac{1}{2}$ cup (125 mL) butter, fill a liquid measuring cup with $\frac{1}{2}$ cup (125 mL) cold water. Add butter until the water level reaches the 1 cup (250 mL) mark. This ensures that you have exactly $\frac{1}{2}$ cup (125 mL) butter.

Use measuring spoons for small amounts of both liquid and dry ingredients. Fill to the top, then level off.

SIFT AS REQUIRED

Some ingredients such as confectioner's (icing) sugar, cocoa powder and cake flour need to be sifted before being blended with other ingredients. If you don't have
a sifter, a fine sieve will do. To ease cleanup, place a piece of waxed paper on the counter. Fill the sieve with the ingredients to be sifted and tap until all have sifted through to the paper. Using the paper as a funnel, transfer the dry ingredients to the rest of the mixture.

ENSURE INGREDIENTS ARE AT THE RIGHT TEMPERATURE

Ingredients should be at room temperature unless otherwise specified. Eggs and cold butter should be removed from the refrigerator at least 1 hour before baking. (If you're short of time, place eggs in a bowl of warm water for 5 minutes. You can soften cold butter in the microwave for a few seconds, but watch very carefully, as butter that is too soft will not cream effectively. You can also cut cold butter into small chunks and beat for a minute or two with an electric mixer to make it the right consistency for creaming.)

One secret to baking tender, flaky pastry is to ensure that all ingredients, including flour, are cold. (See Perfect Pie Crust and Pastry, page 21.)

MIX CAREFULLY

Attention to mixing is as important to baking success as accurate measurement. For best results:

- Combine dry ingredients such as flour, baking soda, baking powder and salt in a bowl and mix together until they are well blended.
- Cream butter and sugar long enough to ensure that the mixture has achieved maximum aeration. It should be light and fluffy. Often a creamed mixture of butter, sugar and eggs will look curdled, but this will correct itself once the flour is added.
- When combining sugar and eggs, beat the mixture until it increases in volume and falls in a ribbon when dropped from a spoon, unless the recipe specifies otherwise.
- Carefully fold lighter ingredients, such as beaten egg whites or whipped cream, into heavier ones to maintain the aeration.
- Mix muffin and quick bread batter very lightly to avoid dense, tough results. Do not worry about small lumps; they will disappear during baking.
- Place mixing bowl on a folded, damp towel to prevent it from slipping.

ROLL WISELY

To keep cookie and pastry dough tender, roll out using a pastry cloth and stockinet-covered rolling pin. By reducing the amount of flour required to prevent the dough from sticking, this technique helps to enhance tenderness.

BAKE ATTENTIVELY

Unless otherwise specified, the recipes in this book were developed using metal pans.

- Reduce the oven temperature by 25°F (10°C) if using glass pans instead of metal.
- Bake cakes, muffins, cookies and quick breads on the middle oven rack. Bake yeast breads and pies on the lower rack unless otherwise specified.
- Always test baked goods for doneness 5 to 10 minutes before the end of the recommended baking time to allow for oven variances.

FREEZING

To store baked goods in the freezer, wrap tightly in plastic wrap and place in sealed containers or freezer bags. When thawing, remove from freezer and thaw in sealed container or bag. This ensures that the moisture lost during freezing will be reabsorbed when the goods have thawed.

Making Perfect Cakes

Many people find baking cakes intimidating as they require particularly close attention to detail. To achieve their lift, cakes, more than most other baked desserts, depend upon the exact proportion of ingredients, often combined with aerating techniques such as creaming or beating egg whites. Even so, cakes need not be daunting; there are many techniques you can use to ensure cake-baking success.

Many cooks find that using cake flour, which is made from a softer wheat than all-purpose flour, improves results. Because Robin Hood Best For Cake & Pastry Flour is lower in protein, it produces cakes with a softer, more delicate crumb. When substituting Robin Hood Best For Cake & Pastry Flour for Robin Hood All-Purpose Flour, replace 1 cup (250 mL) Robin Hood All-Purpose Flour with 1 cup plus 2 tablespoons (280 mL) Robin Hood Best For Cake & Pastry Flour.

MIXING AND BAKING

The following tips will foster cake-baking success:

- To maximize the volume in cakes, ensure that all ingredients are at room temperature.

- To help keep raisins, nuts, chocolate chips and candied fruit suspended in the batter, chop them finely (or use mini chocolate chips) and toss them in about 1 tbsp (15 mL) flour before adding to the batter. Otherwise, they may sink as cake batters are not stiff enough to suspend them.

- Bake a cake as soon as it is mixed as the leavening will start to work once it is moistened. A delay in baking after mixing will result in poor volume.

- Do not use butter, margarine or oil to grease cake pans or the cake may stick and brown too much. Use shortening or cooking spray.

- Do not use a pan that is smaller in volume than the size recommended as the cake may overflow. Slightly larger is usually safe, although the cake will be shallower and require less baking time.

- To eliminate any large air bubbles that may have formed in the batter, bang most cake pans firmly against the countertop before placing in the oven. Do not do this with angel food cake, sponge cake or cakes containing fruit or nuts.

- Bake cakes on the middle oven rack. For proper heat distribution, cake pans should not touch each other or the sides of the oven during baking.

- Use recommended baking times as a guideline. Always set timer for 5 minutes before the minimum time given to allow for oven variances. As previously noted, ovens are often hotter than the temperature indicated, and cakes can easily be overbaked, especially those high in sugar or baked in a dark pan. It's much safer to add more time in 5-minute segments if the cake isn't done.

Testing for Doneness: When cakes are done, a toothpick, wooden skewer or cake tester inserted in the center of the cake will come out clean. (However, this test won't work for some cakes with "gooey" ingredients.) Another indication that the cake is done is that the top will spring back when lightly touched and the cake will come away from the sides of the pan. For lighter cakes, color is also a good indicator — it should be a nice golden brown.

Removing Cakes from the Pan: Unless the recipe specifies otherwise, after removal from the oven, layer cakes should cool in the pan for 10 minutes. Deeper cakes, such as tube cakes and loaves, should be left for 20 minutes. After the required time has passed, turn the cake out and cool completely on a wire rack. To remove the cake from the pan, run a knife around the edge (and also the center, if baking in a tube pan), then invert, shaking the pan gently to remove the cake. Most cakes are inverted twice so that they finish cooling in the same position (top side up) as they are baked. Bundt and angel food cakes are the two exceptions: After cooling initially for about 20 minutes in the pan, turn out Bundt cakes and finish cooling, fluted side up. Baked angel food cakes should cool completely in the pan. After removing from the oven, immediately turn the baked cake upside down on a funnel, bottle or glass bottom and let cool completely.

GLAZING AND FROSTING

Often there is no right or wrong glaze or frosting for a cake; it is just a matter of personal preference. When you're deciding how to finish your cake, consider both color and flavor. Although we've made suggestions for glazes and frostings in most of the recipes, please treat these as guidelines and feel free to use your imagination.

Glazes differ from frostings because they are usually simple ways to finish a cake (for instance, drizzling with melted chocolate). Frostings are thicker and more complicated to make. Cakes are often glazed while still warm, but butter icings, creams and frostings aren't applied until cakes have completely cooled. We hope the following tips will inspire you to think creatively about how to finish your cakes and help you achieve successful results.

Glazing

- Dusting plain cakes with confectioner's (icing) sugar is the simplest and most calorie-conscious way to finish a cake. Just before serving (otherwise the moisture from the cake will quickly absorb the sugar), place confectioner's (icing) sugar in a fine sieve and tap over the surface of the cake. For an elegant or festive look, place a paper doily over the unfrosted cake, then remove carefully after dusting, leaving a lacy decoration.

- When finishing cakes that are brushed with syrup while warm (usually tube and Bundt cakes), place the cake on a rack set over waxed paper to catch the drips.

- A simple drizzle of melted semi-sweet chocolate is a quick and attractive finish for many cakes.

Frosting

- Frost cakes only after they are completely cool. If desired, place cakes to be frosted in the freezer for about 30 minutes to make them less fragile and easier to frost.

- When frosting, place a bit of frosting on the plate to hold the cake in place. To keep the plate clean, set four strips of waxed paper under the edge of the cake to form a square.

Layer Cakes

- Because layer cakes involve setting one cake on top of another, it may be necessary, if the layers are domed, to slice a bit off the top to make them even before frosting.

- When frosting, place the first cake layer, top side down, on a plate. Spread ½ to ¾ cup (125 to 175 mL) frosting over the layer. Place the second cake layer, top side up, over the frosting. You now have the two flat surfaces together in the center so the cakes will sit evenly. Spread a very thin layer of frosting over the top and sides of cake. This seals in crumbs. Then cover with a second, thicker layer of frosting. You can smooth the surface with a long spatula or make swirls with a small spatula or the back of a spoon. If necessary, chill the cake to firm up the frosting. Carefully remove the waxed paper strips.

STORING CAKES

- Properly wrapped, cakes keep very well. You can refrigerate most cakes for up to a week or freeze them for 4 to 6 months.

- Cool unfrosted cakes completely before freezing. Having a few plain cake layers in the freezer is a bonus. You can thaw, fill and frost in no time when necessary.

- For easy slicing and the best flavor, fruit cakes should be made at least 4 weeks in advance, then wrapped and stored in the refrigerator. Cut with a sharp, thin, nonserrated knife.

THAWING CAKES

- If the frosting on a cake contains either eggs or cream, thaw the cake overnight in the refrigerator. Other cakes may be thawed in this manner, or at room temperature, for about 3 hours.

- When thawing unfrosted cakes to be frosted, leave them covered for approximately three-quarters of the thawing time, then uncover for the remaining time. This allows them to dry out slightly, which makes them easier to frost.

Best-Ever Cookies

Almost everyone loves baking cookies. Because they are so easy, quick and delicious, baking cookies is a great way for novice bakers, including kids, to get their start. Cookies also store well, both after baking and as dough, so you can always have home-baked cookies on hand for unexpected guests or after-school treats. Although cookies are among the simplest things to bake, here are a few tips to help make yours even better.

MIXING AND BAKING

- As too much fat may cause cookies to spread, follow the water displacement method for measuring solid fats accurately (see Measure Accurately, page 14).
- Grease cookie sheets only if the recipe indicates. If the sheet is greased unnecessarily, some cookies will spread too much.
- Cookies made with butter or margarine will spread out more than those made with shortening.
- When making cut and rolled cookies, dip the cookie cutter in flour so it won't stick to the dough, and cut the cookies as close together as possible. Although you can reroll scraps of dough, the less the dough is handled, the more tender your cookies will be.
- Use flat cookie sheets without sides for even baking.
- For crisp cookies, press flat with the bottom of a glass dipped in granulated sugar before baking.
- Place cookies about 2 inches (5 cm) apart on the cookie sheet to allow for spreading.
- When baking, place cookie sheet on the middle rack of your oven. Ensure that the sheet is narrower than the oven rack and that it doesn't touch the sides of the oven, so the heat can circulate properly. For best results, bake only one sheet at a time to ensure that heat circulates properly.
- Since cookies are usually small and bake quickly, pay particular attention to the baking time. Always aim to underbake rather than overbake as cookies continue to bake after they are removed from the oven. Begin checking to see if your cookies are done 5 minutes before the time specified in the recipe as every extra minute can make a big difference.
- For soft, chewy cookies, remove from the oven about two minutes before they are done as they will continue to bake on the hot sheet. If you want crisp cookies, bake longer.

STORING COOKIES

- Cool cookies completely before storing.

- Do not store crisp and soft cookies in the same container. Store crisp cookies in a loosely covered container. Store soft, unfrosted cookies in airtight containers, such as sealed plastic bags, tins, cookie jars or plastic containers with screw-top lids.

- To freeze cookies, place in sealed plastic containers or freezer bags and store for up to 6 months.

Perfect Pie Crust and Pastry

There are few items in baking that inspire more trepidation than pie crust and pastry. Even experienced cooks often shy away from making their own pie crust, and yet once you understand the principles associated with making pastry and learn how to "feel" the dough, you'll be able to sense when it has the proper balance of flour and fat and is the right consistency. When making pie crust and pastry, practice really does make perfect, so if you're a novice, allow yourself a few failures and learn from them. Soon you'll be turning out perfect pies and pastry every time you bake. If in doubt, or if time is critical, try Robin Hood's Flaky or Brodie XXX Pie Crust Mix. All the ingredients are premeasured and blended; you just add the water.

MAKING THE DOUGH

- For tender, flaky pastry, all the ingredients, including the flour, should be cold. Freeze butter and/or shortening for 30 minutes before using. Use ice water to bind the ingredients together.

- Measure the flour and the fat accurately. The variable is the quantity of liquid you add, which depends on how well the fat is integrated into the flour, among other factors.

ROLLING IT OUT

- Use a lightly floured pastry cloth and rolling pin covered with a stockinet to roll out the dough.

- Shape the dough into a ball, then flatten into a disk. Center the disk on a floured cloth and roll away from you, from the center out, rotating the dough, until it is the required size. (Check to ensure that you have rolled the dough to the accurate size by holding the pie plate over the dough.)

- To transfer the rolled dough to the pie plate, roll it onto the rolling pin and lift, positioning it properly over the pie plate. Gently set the crust on the plate, then, using your fingers, push it into the sides of the plate. Trim with scissors or a knife.

BAKING

When baking pies and pastry, you can take a number of simple steps to ensure best results. Here are techniques for improving your pies.

To prevent a baked pie shell from shrinking in the pie plate

- Ease the pastry gently into the plate and press against the edge, being careful not to stretch the dough. Trim the edge 1 inch (2.5 cm) from the rim of the plate. Fold under and flute, hooking the edge over the rim to secure it. Prick the bottom and sides well with a fork.

- Cut a 12-inch (30 cm) circle of parchment or aluminum foil and fit into the pie shell. Fill with pie weights or dried beans (about 4 cups/1L). Bake at 425°F (220°C) for 10 to 15 minutes or until set. Cool slightly. Remove beans. Prick with fork. Bake at 350°F (180°C) for 15 to 20 minutes longer or until golden.

To prevent a soggy bottom crust

- Chill the crust about 20 minutes before filling.

- Brush the crust with lightly beaten egg white, then chill for 15 minutes before filling.

- Bake on the bottom oven rack. For most pies, bake at a high temperature for 10 to 15 minutes, then continue baking at a lower temperature.

- Sprinkle toasted ground nuts on the pastry. Press lightly into dough with the back of a spoon before filling. This also adds a nice flavor.

Glazes to enhance a top crust

- For a shiny, deep golden crust, brush with egg yolk beaten with a little water before baking.

- For a shiny crust, brush with lightly beaten egg white or milk.

- For a sugary, sweet crust, brush lightly with water, then sprinkle with sugar.

Flavor enhancements

- You can enhance a pastry to suit its filling by adding complementary ingredients. For dessert pies, try adding cinnamon, ginger, nutmeg, or lemon or orange zest to the dry ingredients before combining with the fat.

Bars and Squares

These are a popular and, compared with cookies, timesaving way to make bite-sized treats. Instead of shaping each piece individually, they are baked in a pan, then cut into pieces. You can make them as large or as small as you like.

Muffins and Quick Breads

There is nothing quite like a warm muffin or hot scone to start the day. Unlike yeast breads, quick breads are leavened with baking powder and baking soda.

TIPS AND TECHNIQUES
Mix muffin and quick bread batter very lightly to avoid dense, tough results. Do not worry about small lumps; they will disappear during baking.

Muffins
- For fast cleanup, bake muffins in paper cups set in ungreased pans. Alternatively, you can grease muffin tins and bake directly in the tin.
- Use an ice-cream scoop with wire release to scoop batter into muffin pans. This results in a uniform size and nicely shaped top.
- Always fill the tins at least two-thirds full.
- If you have not used all the cups in your pan, fill the empty ones with water before placing the pan in the oven to help the muffins bake more evenly.
- To retain freshness, store muffins in an airtight container. Alternatively, you can wrap them in plastic wrap and freeze. When thawing, leave plastic on and bring to room temperature.

Quick Breads
- It is normal for some quick breads to have a lengthwise crack on top of the loaf, so don't worry if this happens to you.
- If your product is soggy and fallen in the middle, the dough may have had too much liquid in proportion to the dry ingredients. If it is coarsely textured, it may have had too much fat.
- Quick breads, such as banana, date and nut and lemon loaves, are delicious sliced and toasted.

Yeast Bread

Not only is homemade bread one of life's great pleasures, it is the epitome of domesticity. Few things taste quite as good as a crusty loaf fresh from the oven or smell as appetizing as the yeasty aroma of baking bread wafting through the house. And bread is a very versatile food. It can be eaten on its own, as an accompaniment to a meal or toasted for breakfast in the morning. It is also very satisfying to make. Many people find the act of kneading dough to be a comforting way of dealing with the frustrations of daily life.

KNOW YOUR INGREDIENTS

Flour is key when making bread. Although you can make excellent bread using Robin Hood All-Purpose Flour, Robin Hood Best For Bread Flour has been specially formulated for baking bread, not only from scratch but also in a bread machine. It will produce breads that are higher in volume with a lighter, more even texture. It is milled from hard wheat only and is specially designed for yeast baking. Feel free to replace Robin Hood All-Purpose Flour with an equivalent amount of Robin Hood Best For Bread Flour in any yeast bread recipe.

Yeast is the ingredient that gives bread its voluminous rise. Although working with yeast isn't tricky, it does require attention to detail. Store your yeast in a cool, dry place and always check the best before date prior to using. Using yeast that has passed its peak can limit how much your bread will rise.

Sugar has a role. In addition to adding flavor to breads and a golden color to the crust, sugar is quick food for the yeast. It helps it to produce the carbon dioxide gas that allows the yeast to activate. However, too much sugar can slow down the yeast action or prevent it from activating.

Other sweeteners can be used if desired. When baking fancy or whole grain breads, you can substitute brown sugar, molasses or honey for granulated sugar if you're feeling like a change. However, you may need to adjust your recipe if substituting a liquid for a dry ingredient.

Fats are important. Fats such as butter, margarine, shortening and oil help to improve the flavor, tenderness and quality of the bread. They also have a lubricating effect on the gluten's meshwork. In other words, adding fats will permit your dough to stretch more easily. Do not substitute oil for butter or margarine when baking bread. Oil is a "liquid" ingredient and butter is a solid. Adjustments in dry and/or liquid ingredients would be necessary to achieve the correct dough consistency.

MAXIMIZE THE POTENTIAL OF YOUR INGREDIENTS

- To achieve a supple, more elastic consistency, carefully measure the wet and dry ingredients. If the dough appears too wet, knead in more flour, a little at a time. If the dough appears too dry, knead in 1 tbsp (15 mL) of liquid at a time. If given a choice, start with a soft dough and add flour as it is much easier to knead flour into dough than a liquid.

- Test to see if your dough has enough flour when you are kneading. Slap your open hand against the ball of dough. If your hand comes away clean, the dough has enough flour. Also, if the dough is sticking to the kneading surface, knead in a little more flour, as required.

- There are different ways of kneading dough. Dough can be kneaded in a mixer with a dough hook, by hand, or by using a combination of these methods. You can also skip this process by using a bread machine.

- To knead dough by hand, turn it out on a lightly floured surface. Kneading is a repetitive process of folding the dough and pushing down on it using the heels of your hands until the appropriate consistency is achieved.

- Allow dough to rise in a warm place (75° to 85°F/24° to 29°C) and away from drafts that can inhibit rising.

- Several factors can affect the volume of bread. Too much or too little flour or salt will inhibit the gluten's performance and the dough will not rise to its full potential. To test if dough has sufficiently risen on the first rise, insert your fingers into the dough. If an indentation remains, it is ready to punch down. If not, allow the dough to rise for a longer period.

- To prevent your loaf of bread from sinking in the middle, do not allow the dough to rise too much. (Remember, it will rise more during baking.) Only allow dough to rise until it has doubled in volume. Otherwise, it may collapse in the oven during baking.

- When shaping loaves, you can eliminate large air bubbles by rolling out the dough on a floured board. Roll the dough into a rectangle approximately 9 by 12 inches (23 by 30 cm), then beginning with a shorter side, roll up jelly roll–style, sealing the roll with the heel of your hand after each turn.

BAKE FOR SUCCESS

- Use shortening to grease your pans. Butter or oil can cause the bread to stick to the pan or burn.

- Since aluminum pans reflect rather than transmit heat, they can result in a lighter-colored loaf. For a darker loaf, try using a baking pan made from something other than aluminum.

- For a different look, try baking loaves free-form on a baking sheet sprinkled with cornmeal or greased. Cornmeal will prevent the bread from sticking and give it an interesting texture.

- Position pans in the oven so that the air can circulate between them and they are evenly exposed to the oven temperature. Bread should be baked on a lower rack in the oven unless otherwise directed. If the crust is becoming too brown, cover the pan loosely with aluminum foil for the duration of the baking time.

- Doughs made with water generally yield a crispier crust than those made with milk. To achieve a crisp crust, spritz the loaf with water during baking. For a darker, richer color, brush with an egg wash before baking or brush finished loaves lightly with butter or margarine and return to the oven for 5 to 10 minutes.

- Too much flour, or too little sugar or fat, can toughen your crust. To soften a crust, brush the loaf with melted butter as soon as it comes out of the oven.

STORE BREADS APPROPRIATELY

- For a crisp crust, keep bread in a paper bag for up to 2 days. Do not wrap bread in plastic unless you want an especially soft crust. Store at room temperature or freeze (refrigeration tends to dry bread). To freshen, heat unwrapped bread in a 350°F (180°C) oven for 10 to 15 minutes.

- Allow bread to cool completely before freezing. Frozen bread keeps and freshens well. To freeze, allow a loaf to cool before placing it in a freezer bag. Remove all of the air from the bag or ice crystals will form during the freezing process. Thaw frozen bread inside the plastic freezer bag so it can absorb the moisture lost during the freezing process. To freshen previously frozen bread, place the thawed loaf on a baking sheet and heat for 10 to 15 minutes at 350°F (180°C).

Bread Machines

Bread machines take all the work out of bread baking but still allow you to enjoy the wonderful aroma and taste of homemade bread. You can make bread from start to finish in the machine or you can prepare the dough in the machine, then remove it, shaping as desired, completing the second rising and baking in a conventional oven. This allows you to make many different varieties of bread such as focaccia, pizza crust, rolls, coffee cakes and so on.

KNOW YOUR SETTINGS

- The Crust Color setting allows you to choose a light, medium or dark crust by slightly varying the baking time or temperature. The higher your machine temperature and the longer the baking time, the darker the crust.

- The Sweet Dough setting is for breads with a higher sugar content, which tend to brown easily and rise slowly. This setting features a longer rising time and lower baking temperature. Use the Light Crust Color setting on your machine if you do not have a Sweet Dough setting.

- The Whole Wheat setting features a longer rising time and is designed to efficiently knead whole grain flours, which are heavier than refined flours. Use this setting for grainy breads as well.

- Use the Dough Cycle/Manual Cycle setting to make rolls, breadsticks, pizza dough or any breads that require hand shaping. This setting will mix, knead and allow dough to rise only once. The beep is your cue to remove the dough from the machine and begin hand shaping. Then let the bread rise in a warm place and bake in a conventional oven.

- The Raisin/Nut Cycle setting is designed to accommodate extra ingredients such as fruits, nuts and vegetables. Adding ingredients too late will not allow enough time for them to fold into the dough and they may clump together. Draining or dusting extra ingredients with flour or cinnamon first will help them separate and mix into the dough.

- When using the Delay Timer Cycle, place the ingredients in the bread pan as directed by the manufacturer. Do not use the delay timer for breads containing perishables (such as eggs and fresh milk), which can spoil in less than two hours.

- Never use metal utensils to remove bread from the pan. These will scratch the nonstick surface.

- To make cleanup easier, grease the dough beater shaft with shortening, or coat it with cooking spray. Soaking the beater in warm water for a few minutes after removing the bread will help to loosen any baked-on ingredients.

Baking at High Altitudes

When baking at altitudes above 3,000 feet (915 m), you may need to adjust baking times and/or temperatures, or fine-tune your recipe in other ways. The higher the altitude, the more the leavening gases in breads and cakes expand. Because water and other liquids boil at lower temperatures (which means that the internal heat needed to cook food takes more time to develop because the food is being cooked at a lower temperature), they also evaporate more quickly. If you are baking at a high altitude, you'll want to make sure that your cakes, breads, muffins and cookies are the best they can be, so please read the following tips carefully.

CAKE RECIPE ADJUSTMENT GUIDE FOR HIGH ALTITUDES

OVEN TEMPERATURE
Increase by 75°F (25°C) to compensate for faster rising in the oven and slower heating.

LIQUIDS
Based on altitude, for each cup (250 mL) increase liquids by the amount indicated below.

Altitude	Increase Liquids By
more than 3,000 feet (915 m)	1 tbsp (15 mL)
5,000 feet (1,525 m)	2 to 3 tbsp (30 to 45 mL)
8,000 feet (2,440 m)	3 to 4 tbsp (45 to 60 mL)

SUGAR
Based on altitude, for each cup (250 mL) decrease sugar by the amount indicated below.

Altitude	Decrease Sugar By
3,000 feet (915 m)	1 tbsp (15 mL)
5,000 feet (1,525 m)	2 to 3 tbsp (30 to 45 mL)
7,000 to 8,000 feet (2,135 to 2,440 m)	3 to 4 tbsp (45 to 60 mL)

FLOUR
Based on altitude, for each cup (250 mL) decrease flour by the amount indicated below.

Altitude	Decrease Flour By
more than 3,000 feet (915 m)	1 tbsp (15 mL)
5,000 feet (1,525 m)	2 tbsp (30 mL)
6,500 feet (1,980 m)	3 tbsp (45 mL)

BAKING POWDER
Based on altitude, for each teaspoon (5 mL) decrease the baking powder by the amount indicated below.

Altitude	Decrease Baking Powder By
more than 3,000 feet (915 m)	$\frac{1}{8}$ tsp (0.5 mL)
5,000 feet (1,525 m)	$\frac{1}{8}$ to $\frac{1}{4}$ tsp (0.5 to 1 mL)
6,500 feet (1,980 m)	$\frac{1}{4}$ tsp (1 mL)

BREADS

At high altitudes, the lower air pressure can cause flour to dry out, water takes longer to boil, and yeast ferments faster, making dough rise more quickly. The following tips can show you how to counteract the effects altitude can have on your finished loaf.

QUICK BREADS

Quick breads vary from muffin-like to cake-like in cell structure. Although the cell structure of biscuits and muffin-type quick breads is firm enough to withstand the increased internal pressure at high altitudes, a bitter or alkaline flavor may result because baking soda or baking powder is not adequately neutralized. In such cases, a slight decrease in the quantity of baking soda or baking powder will usually improve results.

Quick breads with a cake-like texture are more delicately balanced and can usually be improved at high altitudes by following the adjustment recommendations given below for cakes.

CAKES (GENERAL)

Most cake recipes perfected at sea level need no modification up to an altitude of 3,000 feet (915 m). Above that, decreased atmospheric pressure may result in excessive rising, which stretches the cell structure of the cake, making texture coarse, or it breaks the cells — causing cake to fall. This can usually be corrected by decreasing the amount of leavening. Also, increasing the baking temperature 15° to 25°F (5°C to 10°C), "sets" the batter before the cells formed by the leavening gas expand too much.

Fast and excessive evaporation of water at high altitudes leads to a higher concentration of sugar, which weakens the cell structure. To counterbalance this problem, sugar is often decreased and liquid increased.

Only repeated experiments with each recipe can determine the most successful proportion. The accompanying table is a helpful starting point. Try the smaller adjustment first — this may be all that is needed.

Fat, like sugar, weakens the cell structure. Therefore, rich cakes made at high altitudes may also need less fat (1 to 2 tbsp per cup/15 to 30 mL per 250 mL) than when made at sea level. On the other hand, because eggs strengthen cell structure, the addition of an egg may help prevent a "too-rich" cake from falling.

ANGEL FOOD AND SPONGE CAKES

Angel food and sponge cakes present special problems at high altitudes. Since the leavening gas for these cakes is largely air, it is important not to beat too much air into the eggs. They should be beaten only until they form a peak that falls over, not until they are stiff and dry. Overbeating causes the air cells to expand too much and leads to their collapse. By using less sugar and more flour, and increasing the baking temperature, you will also strengthen the cell structure of foam-type cakes.

CAKE MIXES

As the amount of leavening in cake mixes cannot be reduced, when using these products at high altitudes, adjustments usually take the form of strengthening the cell walls of the cake by adding all-purpose flour, possibly an egg yolk (in sponge cake only), and liquid. Suggestions for high-altitude adjustments are provided on most cake mix boxes and these should be followed.

COOKIES

Although many sea-level cookie recipes yield acceptable results at high altitudes, they can often be improved by a slight increase in baking temperature, a slight decrease in baking powder or soda, fat and sugar and/or a slight increase in liquid ingredients and flour. Many cookie recipes contain a higher proportion of sugar and fat than necessary, even at low altitudes.

SUGAR COOKERY

The higher the altitude, the lower the boiling point of liquids and the sooner evaporation begins. Therefore, the cooked-stage temperature for candies, syrups and jellies should be decreased by the difference in the boiling water temperature at your altitude and that of sea level.

PUDDINGS AND CREAM PIE FILLINGS

At altitudes of 5,000 feet (1,525 m) or higher, you may encounter problems if you're using cornstarch as a thickener. You can still achieve good results, as long as the starch is gelatinized to its maximum, which will require the use of direct heat rather than a double boiler as many recipes indicate.

DEEP-FAT FRYING

The lower boiling point of water in foods requires lowering the temperature of the fat to prevent food from overbrowning on the outside while being undercooked on the inside. The decrease varies according to the food being fried, but a rough guide is to lower the frying temperature by about 3°F (16°C) for each increase of 1,000 feet (305 m) in elevation. As an example, at 8,000 feet (2,440 m) croquettes would be fried at 350°F (180°C) instead of 375°F (190°C).

Ingredients

FLOUR

Flour is the most fundamental ingredient in baking. With so many different kinds of flours on the market, it's easy to become confused about what kind to use. Suffice it to say you can use Robin Hood All-Purpose Flour in any of the recipes in this book and achieve excellent results. Robin Hood All-Purpose Flour, which is made from a combination of soft and hard wheat, can be used for all your baking needs, from breads and crusty rolls to cakes, cookies, muffins and pastry.

However, if desired, you can vary recipes by substituting other kinds of flour. You can even mix and match flours if you're so inclined. For instance, try altering the texture of cookies, muffins or quick breads by using half all-purpose and half whole wheat flour in a recipe calling for all-purpose flour. Or for a denser texture and nutty taste, substitute whole wheat flour for the entire amount of all-purpose flour. When making cakes, pastry and other light and tender baked goods, feel free to substitute 1 cup plus 2 tbsp (280 mL) of Robin Hood Best For Cake & Pastry Flour for every cup of all-purpose flour. And when baking yeast breads, you can use 1 cup (250 mL) Robin Hood Best For Bread Flour for every cup (250 mL) of all-purpose flour.

Flour should be kept in a clean, airtight container and stored in a cool, dry place. White flour lasts approximately 1 year, and whole wheat lasts approximately 6 months. To extend the shelf life of flour, store in sealed containers in the refrigerator or freezer.

Unless otherwise specified, sifting flour is unnecessary. Simply spoon flour lightly into a dry measuring cup and level off with a knife. Do not pack down (see Measure Accurately, page 14).

SUGARS

White granulated sugar is the most commonly used sugar in baking. It is free-flowing and doesn't require sifting. Although granulated sugar works well for every baking need, when making shortbreads, superfine or fruit sugar, both of which are readily available in supermarkets, are the best sugars to use.

Confectioner's sugar, which is also known as icing sugar, is first ground to a fine powder, then a small quantity of cornstarch is added to prevent it from lumping and crystallizing. (Be sure to keep the bag airtight.) Confectioner's sugar is used primarily in frostings and glazes. It dissolves almost instantly in liquids, which makes it wonderful for sweetening whipping cream.

When using confectioner's sugar, spoon it into a dry measure, level off, then sift. All the recipes in this book have been based on this method rather than the reverse (sifting then measuring).

Brown sugar is less refined than granulated sugar. The darker the color the more molasses and moisture brown sugar contains and, therefore, the stronger the flavor. Light and dark brown sugars are interchangeable. Brown sugar is often used for toppings, streusels and some frostings. It isn't used much in tender cake batters since it makes them heavier and too moist. However, brown sugar is wonderful in many recipes for cookies and bars, which benefit from the denser texture and caramel flavor.

To measure brown sugar, pack it firmly into a dry measuring cup and level off. Because of its high moisture content, brown sugar tends to lump. Store it in an airtight jar or heavy plastic bag in a cool, dry place. If it does harden, put it in a plastic bag with a slice of apple, seal tightly and set aside for a few days.

OTHER SWEETENERS

Molasses, honey, corn syrup and maple syrup are all effective sweeteners, depending on the recipe used. Molasses, a by-product of refined sugar, is rich and dark and adds flavor and moisture to recipes. It has a strong flavor; if it is not to your liking, you can substitute an equivalent amount of honey, corn syrup or maple syrup.

EGGS

Eggs are indispensable in baking and they play many different roles in recipes. Eggs contribute to leavening, texture, color, flavor, volume and richness in baked goods. They also add nutritional value and act as an emulsifier, binding ingredients together.

All the recipes in this book have been tested using large eggs. When baking, we recommend that you use large eggs.

Always remove eggs from the refrigerator 1 hour before using to allow them to come to room temperature. If the recipe calls for eggs to be separated, do so as soon as you take them from the refrigerator as eggs separate better when they are cold. After separating the yolks from the whites, cover tightly with plastic wrap to prevent drying and leave at room temperature for 1 hour. (This will also help to ensure that you achieve maximum volume after beating the whites.) For food safety reasons, do not leave eggs at room temperature for longer than 1 hour.

Egg replacement products can replace whole eggs in many recipes. Before using, check package information to make sure the product is appropriate for your use.

LEAVENING AGENTS

Yeast is the leavening agent that gives bread its voluminous rise (see page 24 for more on yeast). In these recipes, we have used active dry yeast, bread machine yeast and quick-rise instant yeast.

Active dry yeast is the most common form of yeast available in supermarkets, likely because in addition to being one of the first yeasts made for consumers, it is easy to store and has a relatively long shelf life. Active dry yeast needs to be "proofed," which means it is brought to life when mixed with lukewarm water. To test the vitality of active dry yeast, dissolve 1 tsp (5 mL) sugar in ¼ cup (50 mL) lukewarm water. Sprinkle in yeast and allow to stand for 10 minutes. This is known as "proofing yeast." If the yeast does not bubble within 10 minutes, it is no longer active. One package (¼ oz/8 g) of active dry yeast is equivalent to 2¼ tsp (11 mL).

Quick-rise instant yeast does not require proofing. It is simply mixed with the other dry ingredients. It also takes less time to rise than active dry yeast, as the traditional first rising is replaced by a 15-minute resting period.

Bread machine yeast is specifically designed for use in bread machines. However, it can also be used in all your bread baking. Mix it directly into the dry ingredients.

BAKING SODA

When combined with acids such as yogurt, buttermilk or fruit juice, baking soda creates bubbles of carbon dioxide that cause batter and dough to rise.

BAKING POWDER

Most baking powder begins to work as soon as it is mixed with liquid. Baking powder is baking soda combined with an acid, so it works better as a leavener in batters that are low in acidity. Keep tightly covered in a cool, dry place and replace every 6 months.

DAIRY PRODUCTS

The recipes in this book were tested using 2% **milk** as this is the product most families use. Whole milk (homogenized), low-fat (1%) and non-fat (skim) will also work, although results will vary slightly because of the different fat content. If you're lactose intolerant, substitute an equal amount of lactose-reduced milk.

Buttermilk, which is made from low-fat milk and a bacterial culture, is particularly useful in batters requiring a bit of acidity, where it helps to produce a tender crumb. You can find buttermilk in the dairy case of your supermarket or you can make your own. For 1 cup (250 mL) buttermilk, mix 1 tbsp (15 mL) vinegar or lemon juice with enough milk to make 1 cup (250 mL); let stand for 5 minutes, then stir.

Two kinds of **cream** also appear in some of the recipes in this book: light cream, which has a 10% M.F. (milk fat) content and is also called half-and-half cream, and whipping cream, which has 35% M.F. and is also called heavy cream. Table cream, which has 18% M.F. can be used in recipes calling for light cream, but it should not be substituted in recipes calling for whipping cream.

Evaporated milk is a canned product made by evaporating milk to half its volume. It has a mild caramel taste and comes in whole or low-fat versions. Mixed with an equal amount of water, evaporated milk can be substituted for milk.

Sweetened condensed milk is evaporated milk that has been reduced further and sweetened. It is available in whole and low-fat versions. All the recipes in this book were tested using the whole (or regular) version.

Regular sour cream is about 14% M.F., and all the recipes in this book have been tested using 14% M.F. sour cream. Sour cream is also available in low-fat and no-fat versions. Use regular or low-fat sour cream for baking. We don't recommend the no-fat variety as it can sometimes result in a different texture and quality of baked goods.

Some of the recipes call for **yogurt,** which is available in plain and flavored varieties, with a range of fat contents. As with sour cream, don't use the non-fat type for baking.

Cream cheese is often used in baking, most commonly for cheesecake. These recipes have been tested using full-fat cream cheese. However, you can usually substitute a lower-fat version, if desired. For smooth blending, use blocks of cream cheese that have been softened to room temperature. Do not use tubs of soft, spreadable cream cheese unless specified in the recipe.

CHOCOLATE

Chocolate is a must-have ingredient that no baker should ever be without. Always keep a supply of semi-sweet, bittersweet and unsweetened squares on hand for chopping, grating or melting in recipes. Chocolate chips, which are formulated to soften but hold their shape during baking, should also be a pantry staple. In general, chocolate chips are used in and on top of cakes, while squares are used for melting.

Melting Chocolate

Chocolate is fussy about how it is melted, and if it isn't treated appropriately, it will "seize," leaving you with an unusable glob. However, as long as you follow instructions and ensure that the chocolate does not come in contact with water in the process of melting (it's okay to melt chocolate in a liquid such as cream as long as the hard chocolate is placed in the liquid before the melting process begins) you should be successful.

Basically, chocolate can be melted three different ways. In all cases, coarsely chop the chocolate into pieces before heating. The safest (and slowest) way is to melt the pieces in the top of a double boiler or a bowl set over hot (not boiling) water, stirring frequently, until the chocolate is smooth and melted. Or you can place the pieces in a small saucepan and melt over low heat, stirring constantly, until smooth. Many cooks find a microwave oven useful for this job. Place the chopped chocolate in a microwaveable bowl, cover tightly and heat at Medium power until almost melted, about 1 minute per ounce (28 g). (Times will vary with microwave power.) Remove from oven and stir until the chunks are completely melted.

To make chocolate curls, heat a chocolate square in the microwave for 10 seconds, just until it's warm but not melted. Using a vegetable peeler, shave to make curls.

White chocolate, a blend of sugar, cocoa, butter, milk solids and vanilla, is not really chocolate but has come to be a popular ingredient in baking. It is available in squares and chips.

Cocoa powder is a dry unsweetened powder made from chocolate liquor with most of the cocoa butter removed. Because cocoa tends to clump in storage, it should be measured then sifted before using. If you run out of unsweetened chocolate, 1 oz (28 g) of unsweetened chocolate can be replaced with 3 tbsp (45 mL) cocoa powder plus 1 tbsp (15 mL) butter, margarine or shortening.

NUTS

Nuts add flavor and texture to baked goods. Since they spoil quickly, we recommend that you store nuts in the freezer to keep them fresh. When ready to use, let them thaw and use as directed — or, for optimum flavor, toast them.

To toast nuts: Spread nuts in a single layer on a baking sheet. Bake at 350°F (180°C) for 5 to 10 minutes, stirring often, until golden and fragrant. Chopped nuts will take less time to toast than whole nuts. For hazelnuts, rub off skins in a tea towel while warm. The weight equivalent of 1 cup (250 mL) lightly toasted nuts is approximately 3.8 oz (100 g).

COCONUT

Like nuts, coconut should be stored in the freezer. It, too, has a nicer flavor when toasted. Flaked or shredded coconut both work well in baking. Sweetened or unsweetened is a matter of choice.

To toast coconut: Spread in a single layer on a cookie sheet. Bake at 350°F (180°C) for about 5 minutes, stirring often, until it begins to brown. Watch carefully, as coconut burns quickly.

FLAVORINGS

Always use pure extracts, not artificial, for flavoring. Although they are more expensive, they produce much better results. Extracts and liqueurs should be added to ingredients at room temperature.

SPICES

Spices are an essential ingredient in many recipes, but since they lose their flavor quite quickly, we recommend that you buy them in small amounts. Spices should be stored in tightly sealed glass containers in a cool, dark place and replaced within 6 to 9 months.

DRIED FRUIT

Keep raisins, apricots, cranberries and dates on hand for general baking and buy specialty items such as candied fruit for holiday baking or as needed. Fruits may sink if a batter is not stiff enough. Chopping fruits finely and tossing them in flour to coat will help to keep them suspended in batters.

CANNED FRUIT

Keep a supply of the common types, such as pineapple (crushed, chunks and rings), apricots, peaches and mandarins, in your pantry. Be aware that the proportion of solid fruit to liquid will vary from brand to brand, as will the size of fruit pieces, and this may affect the quantity required.

FROZEN FRUIT

Since cranberries are a great addition to many breads and desserts but they can be hard to find during the summer, we recommend that you keep a few bags in your freezer. Other frozen fruits, such as rhubarb and berries, can be purchased as needed.

FRESH FRUIT YIELDS

Often recipes call for a quantity such as 1 tsp (5 mL) lemon zest or 1 cup (250 mL) mashed bananas. To make your baking easier, we've provided some measured yields for fresh fruits commonly used in baking.

MEASURED YIELDS FOR FRESH FRUIT

Lemons
One medium lemon yields about ¼ cup (50 mL) juice and 2 tsp (10 mL) grated zest.

Oranges
Two or three medium oranges yield about 1 cup (250 mL) juice and 3 tbsp (45 mL) grated zest.

Apples
One pound (500 g) or 3 medium apples yield about 2 cups (500 mL) chopped apples.

Bananas
One pound or 2 or 3 large bananas yield about 1 cup (250 mL) mashed bananas.

Strawberries or raspberries
One pound (500 g) contains about 4 cups (1 L) whole, 3 cups (750 mL) sliced or 2 cups (500 mL) crushed berries.

Desserts

Cranberry Strawberry Rhubarb Dessert

Delicious warm with ice cream or whipped cream.

PREHEAT OVEN TO 350°F (180°C) • 13- BY 9-INCH (3.5 L) CAKE PAN, GREASED

Cake

1½ cups	Robin Hood All-Purpose Flour	375 mL	
½ cup	Robin Hood or Old Mill Oats	125 mL	
¼ cup	packed brown sugar	50 mL	
2½ tsp	baking powder	12 mL	
¼ tsp	salt	1 mL	
¼ cup	butter or margarine	50 mL	
1	egg, beaten	1	
¾ cup	milk	175 mL	
6 cups	thinly sliced rhubarb	1.5 L	
6 oz	sweetened dried cranberries (1 cup/250 mL)	170 g	
1	pkg (3 oz/85 g) strawberry-flavored gelatin dessert mix	1	

MAKES ABOUT 12 SERVINGS

TIP: If fresh rhubarb is not available, use frozen. Thaw and pat dry first.

Topping

6 tbsp	butter or margarine	90 mL
1½ cups	granulated sugar	375 mL
⅔ cup	Robin Hood or Old Mill Oats	150 mL
¼ cup	Robin Hood All-Purpose Flour	50 mL
1 tsp	cinnamon	5 mL

1. **Cake:** Combine first five ingredients in mixing bowl. Cut in butter until crumbly. Add egg and milk, stirring until moistened. Spread evenly in prepared pan. Combine rhubarb and cranberries. Sprinkle evenly over cake. Sprinkle powdered gelatin over fruit.

2. **Topping:** Combine all ingredients. Sprinkle over fruit. Bake for 60 minutes or until fruit is tender.

Preparation time: 25 minutes / Baking time: 1 hour / Freezing: not recommended

Strawberry Cheesecake Squares

Nice on a cookie tray as well as for dessert.

PREHEAT OVEN TO 350°F (180°C) • 13- BY 9-INCH (3.5 L) CAKE PAN, GREASED

Crust

2 cups	Robin Hood All-Purpose Flour	500 mL
¾ cup	packed brown sugar	175 mL
¾ cup	finely chopped almonds	175 mL
¾ cup	butter or margarine	175 mL

Filling

2	pkgs (each 8 oz/250 g) cream cheese, softened	2
⅔ cup	granulated sugar	150 mL
2	eggs	2
½ tsp	almond extract	2 mL
1 cup	strawberry jam	250 mL
¾ cup	sliced almonds	175 mL

MAKES ABOUT 36 SQUARES

TIP: Line pan with foil for easy removal of cooled squares.

1. Crust: Combine all ingredients until crumbly. Reserve ¾ cup (175 mL) for topping. Press remainder into prepared pan. Bake for 12 to 15 minutes or until edges are golden.

2. Filling: Beat cream cheese, sugar, eggs and almond extract on medium speed of electric mixture until smooth. Spread evenly over hot crust. Bake for 15 minutes. Stir jam until smooth. Spread over filling. Stir sliced almonds into reserved crumble mixture. Sprinkle over jam. Bake for 15 minutes longer. Cool completely on wire rack. Refrigerate for at least 3 hours or overnight before cutting into squares. Store in refrigerator.

VARIATION: Try raspberry or apricot jam in place of strawberry.

Preparation time: 30 minutes / Baking time: 45 minutes / Refrigeration time: 3 hours or overnight / Freezing: excellent

Raspberry Almond Cream Crêpes

Having a stack of crêpes in your freezer makes entertaining easy.

6-INCH (15 CM) CRÊPE OR FRYING PAN

Crêpe Batter

3	eggs	3
1¼ cups	milk	300 mL
¾ cup	Robin Hood All-Purpose Flour	175 mL
¼ tsp	salt	1 mL
1 tbsp	granulated sugar	15 mL
2 tbsp	vegetable oil	30 mL

Crêpe Filling

1	pkg (8 oz/250 g) cream cheese, softened	1
¼ cup	confectioner's (icing) sugar, sifted	50 mL
½ tsp	almond extract	2 mL
½ cup	ground almonds	125 mL
1 cup	whipping (35%) cream, whipped stiff	250 mL

Raspberry Sauce

1	pkg (15 oz/425 g) frozen whole raspberries in syrup, thawed	1
	Cranberry juice	
⅓ cup	granulated sugar	75 mL
3 tbsp	cornstarch	45 mL
1 tbsp	lemon juice	15 mL

MAKES ABOUT
8 SERVINGS

TIP: To store crêpes, cool completely and stack between waxed paper; enclose in an airtight plastic bag and freeze.

1. Crêpe Batter: Combine all ingredients in blender container; blend, scraping down sides of container once, for about 1 minute or until smooth. OR whisk eggs until light. Gradually add milk alternately with flour, beating until smooth. Beat in salt, sugar and oil. Cover batter and chill for at least 1 hour or overnight. Stir before cooking.

2. Heat lightly greased 6-inch (15 cm) crêpe pan or frying pan. Remove from heat. Spoon in about 2 tbsp (30 mL) batter. Lift and tilt pan to cover bottom with batter. Return to heat. Brown lightly, then turn over and brown other side. Repeat with remaining batter. Cover cooked crêpes and keep warm if using immediately or cool completely, then stack between waxed paper and refrigerate or freeze in an airtight container.

3. Crêpe Filling: Beat together cream cheese, confectioner's (icing) sugar and almond extract. Fold in almonds and whipped cream.

4. Raspberry Sauce: Drain raspberries, reserving juice. Add cranberry juice to raspberry juice to make 2 cups (500 mL). Combine sugar, cornstarch and juice in saucepan. Cook over medium heat, stirring constantly, until mixture comes to a boil. Stir in lemon juice and raspberries. Keep warm or cool to room temperature.

5. Assembly: Fill crêpes. Roll up. Top with warm or cooled sauce.

VARIATION: Try strawberries instead of raspberries.

Preparation time: 40 minutes / Refrigeration time: 1 hour / Cooking time: 30 minutes / Sauce: 10 minutes

Mix 'n' Match
Ice Cream Dessert

*The variety is endless. Use your favorite ice cream and sundae sauce
for an effortless dessert.*

PREHEAT OVEN TO 400°F (200°C) • 13- BY 9-INCH (3.5 L) CAKE PAN, GREASED

1½ cups	Robin Hood All-Purpose Flour	375 mL	**MAKES ABOUT 15 SERVINGS**
1 cup	Robin Hood or Old Mill Oats	250 mL	
1 cup	chopped pecans	250 mL	**TIP:** Thaw 10 minutes before serving to soften slightly for easy cutting.
½ cup	packed brown sugar	125 mL	
1 cup	butter or margarine, melted	250 mL	
1 cup	butterscotch or chocolate chips	250 mL	
1½ cups	butterscotch or chocolate sundae sauce	375 mL	
8 cups	ice cream, softened	2 L	

1. Combine first four ingredients in large bowl. Stir in melted butter. Mix well. Spread evenly on large baking sheet with sides. Bake, stirring occasionally, for 20 to 25 minutes or until golden. Crumble while warm; cool completely.

2. Press half of the oat mixture into prepared pan. Stir chips into remaining oat mixture. Drizzle half of the sauce over crumbs in pan. Spread with softened ice cream. Drizzle remaining sauce over ice cream. Cover with butterscotch chip crumb mixture. Cover and freeze. Cut into pieces as needed.

VARIATION: Try vanilla, butterscotch ripple, cherry, strawberry or chocolate ice cream. Almost any flavor is great.

Preparation time: 15 minutes / Baking time: 25 minutes / Freezing: necessary

Lemon-Glazed Cheesecake Squares

A lemon lover's delight.

PREHEAT OVEN TO 350°F (180°C)
13- BY 9-INCH (3.5 L) CAKE PAN, GREASED

Crust

2 cups	Robin Hood All-Purpose Flour	500 mL
½ cup	confectioner's (icing) sugar, sifted	125 mL
1 cup	butter	250 mL

Filling

3	pkgs (each 8 oz/250 g) cream cheese, softened	3
¾ cup	granulated sugar	175 mL
3	eggs	3
⅓ cup	lemon juice	75 mL
2 tsp	vanilla	10 mL

Topping

2 cups	sour cream	500 mL
3 tbsp	granulated sugar	45 mL

Glaze

½ cup	granulated sugar	125 mL
2 tbsp	cornstarch	30 mL
¾ cup	water	175 mL
⅓ cup	lemon juice	75 mL
1	egg yolk, beaten	1
1 tbsp	butter	15 mL

MAKES ABOUT
12 SERVINGS

TIP: Prepare a day ahead for convenience and optimum texture and flavor.

1. Crust: Combine all ingredients in food processor or with pastry blender until crumbly. Press in prepared pan. Bake for 15 to 20 minutes or until light golden.

2. Filling: Beat cream cheese and sugar on high speed of electric mixer until smooth. Add eggs, lemon juice and vanilla, beating until smooth. Spread over crust. Bake for 35 minutes or until set.

3. Topping: Combine sour cream and sugar. Spread over cheesecake. Return to oven for 5 minutes. Cool for 1 hour.

4. Glaze: Combine sugar and cornstarch in saucepan. Stir in water, lemon juice and egg yolk. Cook on medium heat, stirring constantly, until mixture comes to a boil and thickens. Stir in butter. Cool slightly. Spread over cheesecake. Store in refrigerator. Cut into squares.

VARIATION: Top each square with a small piece of fruit.

**Preparation time: 30 minutes / Baking time: 1 hour /
Refrigeration time: 1 hour / Freezing: not recommended**

Deep-Fried Apple Rings

Serve warm with ice cream and maple syrup for a yummy dessert.

PREHEAT OIL TO 375°F (190°C) • DEEP-FRYER

1 cup	Robin Hood All-Purpose Flour	250 mL	MAKES ABOUT 3 DOZEN RINGS
2 tbsp	cornstarch	30 mL	
1 tbsp	granulated sugar	15 mL	
½ tsp	baking powder	2 mL	**TIP:** Brush peeled apples with lemon juice to prevent browning.
½ tsp	salt	2 mL	
1	egg	1	
1 cup	milk	250 mL	
½ cup	granulated sugar	125 mL	
½ tsp	cinnamon	2 mL	
5	medium apples	5	
	Oil or shortening for deep-frying		

1. Combine flour, cornstarch, 1 tbsp (15 mL) sugar, baking powder and salt in mixing bowl. Set aside.

2. Beat together egg and milk. Add to dry ingredients and whisk until well blended. Refrigerate for 1 hour.

3. Mix together ½ cup (125 mL) sugar and cinnamon. Set aside. Peel and core apples. Cut crosswise into ¼-inch (5 mm) thick rings.

4. Heat 2 to 3 inches (5 to 8 cm) oil in deep-fryer. Dip apple slices in batter, allowing excess to drip back into bowl. Fry two to three at a time in hot oil, turning frequently, for 3 to 4 minutes or until golden brown. Drain on paper towels. Roll in cinnamon-sugar mixture. Serve warm.

Preparation time: 20 minutes / Refrigeration time: 1 hour / Frying time: 4 minutes per batch

Mixed Berry Cheese Torte

A not-too-sweet dessert that tastes as great as it looks.

PREHEAT OVEN TO 350°F (180°C) • 10-INCH (25 CM) SPRINGFORM PAN, GREASED

Crust

1¾ cups	Robin Hood All-Purpose Flour	425 mL	
½ cup	granulated sugar	125 mL	
½ tsp	baking powder	2 mL	
½ tsp	baking soda	2 mL	
¼ tsp	salt	1 mL	
¾ cup	butter, softened	175 mL	
2	eggs	2	
1 tsp	vanilla	5 mL	

Filling

1	pkg (8 oz/250 g) cream cheese, softened	1
1	egg	1
¼ cup	granulated sugar	50 mL
1	can (19 oz/540 mL) mixed berry pie filling, divided	1

MAKES ABOUT 12 SERVINGS

TIP: For an attractive presentation, sift confectioner's (icing) sugar on top just before serving.

1. **Crust:** Combine all ingredients in large bowl of electric mixer. Beat at medium speed for about 2 minutes or until smooth. Spread over bottom and 2 inches (5 cm) up side of prepared pan.

2. **Filling:** Beat together cream cheese, egg and sugar in small bowl at medium speed until smooth and creamy. Reserve ¾ cup (175 mL) of the pie filling for top. Spread remainder over prepared crust. Pour cheese mixture evenly on top. Spoon reserved pie filling evenly over cheese mixture. Bake for 45 to 55 minutes or until set and light golden brown. Serve slightly warm or cool.

Preparation time: 25 minutes / Baking time: 55 minutes / Freezing: excellent

Chocolate Strawberry Mousse Delight

Prepare a day ahead for easy entertaining.

PREHEAT OVEN TO 350°F (180°C) • 9-INCH (23 CM) SPRINGFORM PAN, GREASED

Chocolate Base

½ cup	shortening	125 mL	
3	squares (each 1 oz/28 g) unsweetened chocolate	3	
1¼ cups	granulated sugar	300 mL	
1 tsp	vanilla	5 mL	
3	eggs	3	
⅔ cup	Robin Hood All-Purpose Flour	150 mL	
½ tsp	baking powder	2 mL	

Topping

1	pkg (15 oz/425 g) frozen sliced strawberries in syrup, thawed	1	
1	envelope (1 tbsp/15 mL) unflavored gelatin	1	
½ cup	granulated sugar	125 mL	
2 tbsp	lemon juice	30 mL	
2 cups	whipping (35%) cream, divided	500 mL	
	Fresh strawberries		

MAKES ABOUT 8 SERVINGS

TIP: Desserts containing gelatin and whipped cream don't freeze well.

1. Chocolate Base: Melt shortening and chocolate in saucepan over low heat, stirring until smooth. Remove from heat. Add sugar, vanilla and eggs. Mix well. Combine flour and baking powder. Add to chocolate mixture, stirring until well blended. Spread in prepared pan. Bake for 22 to 27 minutes or just until set. Cool in pan.

2. Topping: Drain strawberries, reserving liquid. Add enough water to liquid to make 1¼ cups (300 mL). Combine gelatin and sugar in saucepan over medium heat. Stir in strawberry liquid and lemon juice. Bring mixture to a boil, stirring constantly to dissolve sugar and gelatin. Remove from heat. Chill until starting to set, about 1½ hours. Beat 1¼ cups (300 mL) of the whipping cream to stiff peaks. Beat gelatin mixture in small bowl on high speed of electric mixer until light. Fold in whipped cream. Fold in drained strawberries. Spread evenly over base in pan. Refrigerate for 3 hours or until set, or overnight. To serve, beat remaining whipped cream to stiff peaks. Decorate mousse attractively with whipped cream and fresh berries.

VARIATION: Replace strawberries with raspberries.

Preparation time: 30 minutes / Baking time: 27 minutes / Refrigeration time: 1½ hours (gelatin mixture) plus 3 hours or overnight / Freezing: not recommended

Raspberry Angel Dome

A showstopping dessert that's prepared the day before for easy entertaining.

LARGE SERVING BOWL

1	pkg (16 oz/450 g) Robin Hood White Angel Food Cake Mix	1
2	envelopes (each 1 tbsp/15 mL) unflavored gelatin	2
½ cup	granulated sugar	125 mL
1	can (12 oz/341 mL) frozen raspberry juice concentrate, thawed	1
2 cups	water	500 mL
2 cups	whipping (35%) cream, divided	500 mL
1 cup	fresh raspberries, optional	250 mL
¾ cup	flaked coconut, toasted	175 mL

MAKES ABOUT
10 SERVINGS

TIP: Prepare cake and freeze. Simply thaw when needed.

1. Prepare and bake angel food cake mix according to package directions. Cool. Cut cake into 1-inch (2.5 cm) cubes. Set aside. Mix together gelatin and sugar in saucepan. Stir in raspberry juice and water. Bring to a boil, stirring constantly until dissolved. Refrigerate until starting to set. Whip half of the cream to stiff peaks. Beat gelatin mixture on high speed of electric mixer until light. Fold in whipped cream and berries.

2. Line large bowl with plastic wrap. Place one-third of the cake cubes in bowl. Cover with one-third of the gelatin mixture, pressing lightly. Repeat layers twice. Cover and refrigerate overnight. Turn out, rounded side up, onto serving plate. Remove plastic wrap. Whip remaining cream until stiff. Spread evenly over dome. Sprinkle with coconut.

VARIATION: Try other fruit juice concentrates, such as cranberry, pineapple-orange and fruit punch.

Preparation time: 20 minutes / Refrigeration time: overnight / Freezing: not recommended

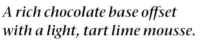

Chocolate Lime Mousse Dessert

A rich chocolate base offset with a light, tart lime mousse.

PREHEAT OVEN TO 350°F (180°C)
10-INCH (25 CM) SPRINGFORM PAN, GREASED

Chocolate Base

½ cup	butter or margarine	125 mL
3	squares (each 1 oz/28 g) unsweetened chocolate	3
1¼ cups	granulated sugar	300 mL
3	eggs	3
⅔ cup	Robin Hood All-Purpose Flour	150 mL
¼ tsp	baking powder	1 mL

Topping

1	envelope (1 tbsp/15 mL) unflavored gelatin	1
½ cup	granulated sugar	125 mL
4	egg yolks	4
½ cup	lime juice	125 mL
2 tsp	grated lime zest	10 mL
4	egg whites	4
½ cup	granulated sugar	125 mL
½ cup	whipping (35%) cream, whipped stiff	125 mL
	Lime slices	

MAKES ABOUT 8 SERVINGS

TIP: Warm limes slightly in microwave to get maximum amount of juice.

1. **Chocolate Base:** Melt butter and chocolate in saucepan over low heat, stirring until smooth. Remove from heat. Add remaining ingredients, stirring until smooth. Spread in prepared pan. Bake for 20 to 25 minutes or just until set. Cool in pan.

2. **Topping:** Combine first four ingredients in small saucepan. Cook, stirring constantly, over medium heat for about 5 minutes or until slightly thickened (it thickens more on cooling). Stir in zest. Refrigerate until mixture starts to set. Beat egg whites and ½ cup (125 mL) sugar to stiff peaks. Fold egg whites and whipped cream into lime mixture gently but thoroughly. Spread over chocolate base. Refrigerate for about 3 hours or until set, or overnight. Decorate with lime slices.

VARIATION: Replace lime juice and zest with lemon.

**Preparation time: 25 minutes / Baking time: 25 minutes /
Refrigeration time: 3 hours or overnight / Freezing: not recommended**

Buttery Apple Torte

A year-round dessert that's easy to make for family and company, too.

PREHEAT OVEN TO 450°F (230°C) • 10-INCH (25 CM) SPRINGFORM PAN, GREASED

Crust

¾ cup	butter, softened	175 mL
½ cup	granulated sugar	125 mL
1⅔ cups	Robin Hood All-Purpose Flour	400 mL
½ cup	apricot or raspberry jam	125 mL

Filling

8 oz	spreadable cream cheese	250 g
¼ cup	granulated sugar	50 mL
1	egg	1
1 tsp	vanilla	5 mL

Topping

3 cups	thinly sliced peeled apples	750 mL
⅓ cup	granulated sugar	75 mL
1 tsp	cinnamon	5 mL
⅓ cup	sliced almonds	75 mL

MAKES ABOUT
8 SERVINGS

TIPS: Toast almonds and sprinkle on torte just before serving to keep them crunchy.

A sprinkling of confectioner's (icing) sugar before serving adds a nice finishing touch.

1. Crust: Cream together butter and sugar. Blend in flour. Working with hands, mix well to form smooth dough. Press evenly onto bottom and 1½ inches (3.5 cm) up sides of prepared pan. Spread jam evenly over crust.

2. Filling: Beat together all ingredients with electric mixer until smooth. Spread carefully over jam.

3. Topping: Toss together apples, sugar and cinnamon to coat apples well. Spoon over filling. Sprinkle with almonds. Bake at 450°F (230°C) for 10 minutes, then reduce heat to 400°F (200°C) and bake for 25 to 30 minutes longer or until apples are tender-crisp. Serve warm or cool.

VARIATION: Any flavor of jam works well.

Preparation time: 30 minutes / Baking time: 40 minutes / Freezing: not recommended

Bumbleberry Cobbler

Once a favorite, always a favorite.

PREHEAT OVEN TO 400°F (200°C)
9-INCH (2.5 L) SQUARE CAKE PAN OR 2½-QUART (2.5 L) BAKING DISH, GREASED

Fruit

5 cups	thinly sliced peeled apples	1.25 L
1 cup	fresh or frozen cranberries	250 mL
1 cup	fresh or frozen raspberries	250 mL
¾ cup	granulated sugar	175 mL
¼ cup	Robin Hood All-Purpose Flour	50 mL
⅓ cup	water	75 mL

Topping

1¾ cups	Robin Hood All-Purpose Flour	425 mL
2 tbsp	granulated sugar	30 mL
4 tsp	baking powder	20 mL
½ tsp	salt	2 mL
½ cup	butter or margarine	125 mL
1 cup	milk	250 mL

MAKES ABOUT
6 SERVINGS

TIP: Choose a tart crisp apple like Granny Smith. Decrease water if fruit is juicy.

1. Fruit: Combine all ingredients. Mix well. Spread in prepared pan.
2. Topping: Mix together flour, sugar, baking powder and salt. Cut in butter with pastry blender until mixture resembles coarse meal. Add milk all at once. Stir with fork until all ingredients are moistened. Drop spoonfuls of batter over fruit, covering surface. Place pan on piece of foil to catch any drips that boil over. Bake for 25 to 30 minutes or until top is golden. Serve warm.

VARIATION: Try other fruit mixtures, keeping total amount the same.

Preparation time: 25 minutes / Baking time: 30 minutes / Freezing: not recommended

Pies and Pastries

Prize-Winning Pecan Pie

Top with a dollop of whipped cream or a scoop of vanilla ice cream.

PREHEAT OVEN TO 425°F (220°C) • 9-INCH (23 CM) PIE PLATE

1	envelope Robin Hood Flaky or Brodie XXX Pie Crust Mix	1
1 cup	pecan halves	250 mL
3	eggs	3
⅔ cup	granulated sugar	175 mL
Pinch	salt	Pinch
1 cup	corn syrup	250 mL
⅓ cup	butter, melted	75 mL

MAKES ABOUT
8 SERVINGS

TIP: Keep nuts right side up for the nicest appearance.

1. Prepare pastry according to package directions for unbaked 9-inch (23 cm) pie shell using half the dough (reserve remaining pastry for future use).

2. Spread pecans over pastry. Combine eggs, sugar, salt, corn syrup and melted butter. Beat well. Pour over pecans. Bake on lower oven rack at 425°F (220°C) for 10 minutes, then reduce temperature to 350°F (180°C) and bake for 25 to 30 minutes longer or just until set. Cool.

Preparation time: 20 minutes / Baking time: 40 minutes / Freezing: excellent

Peach 'n' Cranberry Apple Pie

A flavorful twist on an all-time favorite.

PREHEAT OVEN TO 450°F (230°C) • 9-INCH (23 CM) PIE PLATE

Crust

1	envelope Robin Hood Flaky or Brodie XXX Pie Crust Mix	1	MAKES ABOUT 6 SERVINGS

Filling

¾ cup	granulated sugar	175 mL	**TIP:** Brush top pastry with milk and sprinkle with sugar before baking.
¼ cup	Robin Hood All-Purpose Flour	50 mL	
1 tsp	cinnamon	5 mL	
¼ tsp	nutmeg	1 mL	
4 cups	sliced peeled apples	1 L	
2 cups	fresh or canned sliced peaches, drained	500 mL	
1 cup	cranberries, fresh or frozen	250 mL	
1 tbsp	lemon juice	15 mL	
2 tbsp	butter	30 mL	

1. Crust: Prepare pastry according to package directions for two-crust pie. Roll out bottom crust and fit into pie plate.
2. Filling: Mix together sugar, flour, cinnamon and nutmeg. Combine sugar mixture with apples, peaches, cranberries and lemon juice. Mix well. Fill bottom crust with fruit mixture. Dot with butter. Place top pastry crust over filling. Seal and flute edge. Slash top crust for steam to escape. Place pie on piece of foil to catch any drips. Bake on lower oven rack at 450°F (230°C) for 15 minutes, then reduce temperature to 350°F (180°C) and bake for 35 to 40 minutes longer or until fruit is tender and crust is golden.

VARIATION: Replace cranberries with blueberries.

Preparation time: 25 minutes / Baking time: 55 minutes / Freezing: excellent

Light and Lemony Cream Pie

Smooth, light and refreshing.

PREHEAT OVEN TO 450°F (230°C) • 9-INCH (23 CM) PIE PLATE

Crust

1	envelope Robin Hood Flaky or Brodie XXX Pie Crust Mix	1	
2	squares (each 1 oz/28 g) bittersweet chocolate, melted	2	

Filling

1	envelope (1 tbsp/15 mL) unflavored gelatin	1
½ cup	granulated sugar	125 mL
Pinch	salt	Pinch
4	egg yolks	4
½ cup	lemon juice	125 mL
1 tbsp	grated lemon zest	15 mL
4	egg whites	4
½ cup	granulated sugar	125 mL
½ cup	whipping (35%) cream, beaten stiff	125 mL
	Lemon slices to garnish, optional	

MAKES ABOUT
8 SERVINGS

TIP: A thin layer of melted chocolate on a baked pie shell will keep the crust from getting soggy. It also adds a nice flavor but isn't a necessity.

1. Crust: Prepare pastry according to package directions for one-crust pie. Crimp edges. Prick well. Refrigerate for 1 hour. Bake for 12 to 15 minutes or until golden. Cool completely. (Wrap and refrigerate remaining pastry for later use.) Spread melted chocolate evenly over pastry shell. Cool.

2. Filling: Combine gelatin, ½ cup (125 mL) sugar, salt, egg yolks and lemon juice in small saucepan. Cook, stirring constantly, over medium heat for about 6 minutes or until slightly thickened. (It thickens more on cooling.) Stir in zest. Refrigerate just until mixture starts to set, about 30 minutes. Beat egg whites and ½ cup (125 mL) sugar to stiff peaks. Fold egg whites and whipped cream into lemon mixture gently but thoroughly. Pile into baked pie shell. Refrigerate for about 2½ hours or until set, or overnight. Decorate with lemon slices, if desired.

VARIATION: Use white or semi-sweet chocolate to spread on the crust.

Preparation time: 30 minutes / Baking time: 15 minutes / Cooking time: 6 minutes / Refrigeration time: 1 hour (crust) plus 3 hours (filling) / Freezing: not recommended

Upside-Down Apple Pecan Pie

A novel twist on an old-fashioned favorite.

PREHEAT OVEN TO 425°F (220°C) • 9-INCH (23 CM) PIE PLATE

Glaze

¼ cup	packed brown sugar	50 mL
1 tbsp	butter, melted	15 mL
1 tbsp	corn syrup	15 mL
½ cup	pecan halves	125 mL

Crust

1	envelope Robin Hood Flaky or Brodie XXX Pie Crust Mix	1

Filling

⅔ cup	granulated sugar	150 mL
3 tbsp	Robin Hood All-Purpose Flour	45 mL
1 tsp	cinnamon	5 mL
5 cups	sliced peeled apples	1.25 L

MAKES ABOUT
8 SERVINGS

TIPS: Place pie on foil or baking sheet to catch any juice that may run over.

Serve warm with ice cream or whipped cream.

1. Glaze: Combine brown sugar, melted butter and corn syrup in pie plate. Spread evenly to coat bottom of pan. Arrange pecans over top.

2. Crust: Prepare pastry according to package directions for two-crust pie. Place bottom pastry over mixture in pan, gently pressing onto nuts.

3. Filling: Combine all ingredients. Turn into pastry-lined pan. Cover with top pastry. Fold edge under bottom crust. Press together to seal. Flute edges. Cut slits to allow steam to escape. Bake on lower oven rack at 425°F (220°C) for 10 minutes, then reduce temperature to 325°F (160°C) and bake for 25 to 35 minutes longer or until apples are tender. Let set for 5 minutes, then loosen edge of pie and carefully invert onto serving plate.

Preparation time: 30 minutes / Baking time: 45 minutes / Freezing: not recommended

Lemon Tart

If you like lemon, you'll love this.

PREHEAT OVEN TO 375°F (190°C) • 9-INCH (23 CM) FLAN PAN WITH REMOVABLE SIDES

Crust

1 cup	Robin Hood All-Purpose Flour	250 mL
¼ cup	granulated sugar	50 mL
¼ cup	butter	50 mL
1	egg, beaten	1

Filling

3	eggs	3
½ cup	granulated sugar	125 mL
1 tbsp	grated lemon zest (1 to 2 lemons)	15 mL
1 cup	lemon juice (3 to 4 lemons)	250 mL
¾ cup	ground almonds	175 mL
⅓ cup	melted butter, cooled	75 mL
	Fresh berries, optional	

MAKES ABOUT 12 SERVINGS

TIPS: Garnish with fresh berries, if desired.

If you prefer a not-so-tart tart, reduce lemon juice to ¾ cup (175 mL).

1. Crust: Combine flour and sugar. Cut in butter until mixture resembles coarse crumbs. Stir in egg. Working with hands, mix well to form smooth dough. Press into sides and bottom of pan. Prick pastry well with fork. Refrigerate for 30 minutes. Bake on lower oven rack for 10 to 12 minutes. Cool.

2. Filling: Whisk together eggs, sugar, lemon zest and juice. Stir in almonds and cooled melted butter. Pour carefully into pastry shell. Bake for 25 to 30 minutes or until filling is set and pastry is light golden. Cool completely. Serve with fresh berries, if desired.

Preparation time: 20 minutes / Refrigeration time: 30 minutes / Baking time: 42 minutes / Freezing: not recommended

Open Apple Plum Pie

A year-round favorite — especially warm with a scoop of ice cream.

PREHEAT OVEN TO 450°F (230°C) • 9-INCH (23 CM) PIE PLATE

Crust

1	envelope Robin Hood Flaky or Brodie XXX Pie Crust Mix	1	**MAKES ABOUT 8 SERVINGS**

Filling

¾ cup	granulated sugar	175 mL	**TIP:** The lemon juice will prevent apples from turning brown.
⅓ cup	Robin Hood All-Purpose Flour	75 mL	
1 tsp	cinnamon	5 mL	
¼ tsp	nutmeg	1 mL	
5 cups	sliced peeled apples	1.25 L	
2½ cups	sliced plums	625 mL	
1 tbsp	lemon juice	15 mL	
2 tbsp	butter	30 mL	
	Milk and sugar to glaze, optional		

1. **Crust:** Prepare pastry according to package directions for one-crust pie. Wrap and set aside.

2. **Filling:** Combine first seven ingredients. Mix well.

3. Roll out pastry on floured surface into 15-inch (38 cm) circle. Fit into pie plate, allowing pastry to overhang. Fill with fruit mixture. Dot with butter. Fold pastry over fruit, pleating into rough circle. If desired, brush pastry with milk and sprinkle with sugar. Bake on lower oven rack at 450°F (230°C) for 10 minutes, then reduce temperature to 350°F (180°C) and bake for 35 to 45 minutes longer or until crust is golden and fruit is tender.

VARIATION: Replace plums with peaches or apples for another great taste.

Preparation time: 30 minutes / Baking time: 55 minutes / Freezing: not recommended

The Ultimate Butter Tart

If you like runny, gooey tarts, you'll love these. Try them warm with ice cream.

PREHEAT OVEN TO 425°F (220°C) • 12-CUP MUFFIN PAN • 4-INCH (10 CM) CUTTER

Crust

1	envelope Robin Hood Flaky or Brodie XXX Pie Crust Mix	1

Filling

½ cup	packed brown sugar	125 mL
½ cup	corn syrup	125 mL
¼ cup	butter, softened	50 mL
1	egg, lightly beaten	1
1 tsp	vanilla	5 mL
¼ tsp	salt	1 mL
¾ cup	raisins	175 mL

MAKES 12 TARTS

TIP: If you don't have a cookie cutter, use the lid from a large jar.

1. **Crust:** Prepare pastry according to package directions for two-crust pie. Roll out thinly on lightly floured surface. Cut into rounds with 4-inch (10 cm) cutter. Fit into muffin cups.

2. **Filling:** Combine all ingredients except raisins. Mix well. Divide raisins evenly among pastry shells. Fill two-thirds full with syrup mixture. Bake on lower oven rack for 12 to 15 minutes or just until set. Don't overbake. Underbaking makes them runnier. Cool on wire rack, then remove from pans.

VARIATION: Replace raisins with chopped pecans for nut lovers.

Preparation time: 25 minutes / Baking time: 15 minutes / Freezing: excellent

Chewy Cherry Coconut Tarts

The name says it all.

PREHEAT OVEN TO 325°F (160°C) • 12-CUP MUFFIN PAN

Crust

½ cup	butter, softened	125 mL	MAKES 12 TARTS
½ cup	packed brown sugar	125 mL	
1	egg yolk	1	**TIPS:** Work dough with hands to make smooth.
1 cup	Robin Hood All-Purpose Flour	250 mL	

Filling

2	egg whites	2	Use floured fingers to press dough into pan.
½ cup	packed brown sugar	125 mL	Use your favorite kind of nut.
½ cup	flaked coconut	125 mL	
⅓ cup	chopped maraschino cherries, drained	75 mL	
¼ cup	finely chopped nuts	50 mL	
1 tsp	vanilla	5 mL	

1. **Crust:** Combine all ingredients, mixing to form smooth dough. Press into muffin cups to form tart shells.
2. **Filling:** Beat egg whites to stiff peaks. Fold in remaining ingredients until blended. Mix well. Spoon into prepared shells. Bake on lower oven rack for 18 to 23 minutes or until golden. Cool.

Preparation time: 20 minutes / Baking time: 23 minutes / Freezing: excellent

Cakes

Orange Angel Cream Cake

Refreshingly light and creamy — a nice finish to any meal.

PREHEAT OVEN TO 325°F (160°C) • 10-INCH (4 L) TUBE PAN

Cake

1	pkg (16 oz/450 g) Robin Hood Angel Food Cake Mix	1		MAKES ABOUT 12 SERVINGS
1 cup	water	250 mL		
1/3 cup	orange juice	75 mL		**TIP:** Prepare cake ahead and freeze. Thaw and use when needed.
1 tbsp	grated orange zest	15 mL		
2 to 3 drops	orange or yellow food coloring, optional	2 to 3 drops		

Filling & Topping

2 cups	whipping (35%) cream	500 mL
2 tbsp	confectioner's (icing) sugar	30 mL
2 tsp	grated orange zest	10 mL
	Mandarin orange segments, optional	

1. Cake: Combine all ingredients in large bowl. Beat on low speed of electric mixer for 30 seconds, then on medium speed for 1 minute. Pour into tube pan. Bake for 50 to 60 minutes. Place upside down to cool completely, then remove from pan. Cut horizontally into three layers.

2. Filling & Topping: Beat cream and confectioner's sugar to stiff peaks. Fold in zest. Spread between layers and on top of cake. Garnish with mandarins, if desired. Chill until serving.

Preparation time: 20 minutes / Baking time: 1 hour / Freezing: not recommended

Cranberry Apple Cake

This cake is nice frosted, plain or simply sprinkled with confectioner's sugar.

PREHEAT OVEN TO 325°F (160°C) • 10-INCH (4 L) TUBE PAN, GREASED AND FLOURED

Cake

1¼ cups	vegetable oil	300 mL
1¼ cups	granulated sugar	300 mL
½ cup	packed brown sugar	125 mL
4	eggs	4
3 cups	Robin Hood All-Purpose Flour	750 mL
2 tsp	cinnamon	10 mL
1 tsp	baking soda	5 mL
1 tsp	baking powder	5 mL
¾ tsp	salt	3 mL
½ tsp	nutmeg	2 mL
3½ cups	diced peeled apples	875 mL
6 oz	dried cranberries (1 cup/250 mL)	170 g

Frosting

¼ cup	packed brown sugar	50 mL
2½ tbsp	light (10%) cream	35 mL
2 tbsp	butter	30 mL
⅔ cup	confectioner's (icing) sugar (approx)	150 mL

MAKES ABOUT 12 SERVINGS

TIP: Store dried cranberries in the freezer to retain their soft, moist texture.

1. **Cake:** Beat oil, sugars and eggs in large mixing bowl. Combine next six dry ingredients. Add to batter along with apples and cranberries, stirring until moistened. Spread in prepared pan. Bake for about 1½ hours or until toothpick inserted in center comes out clean. Cool for 20 minutes in pan, then transfer to wire rack and cool completely.

2. **Frosting:** Heat first three ingredients in saucepan over medium heat, stirring until sugar is dissolved and mixture comes to a boil. Cool to room temperature. Add enough confectioner's sugar to make a drizzling consistency, beating until smooth. Drizzle over cake. Decorate as desired.

Preparation time: 15 minutes /
Baking time: 1½ hours / Freezing: excellent

Lemon Poppy Seed Layer Cake

The lemon lover's dream dessert. The crunch of poppy seeds adds an interesting texture to cakes.

PREHEAT OVEN TO 350°F (180°C)
TWO 9-INCH (1.5 L) ROUND CAKE PANS, GREASED AND FLOURED

Cake

2 cups	Robin Hood All-Purpose Flour or 2¼ cups (550 mL) Robin Hood Best For Cake & Pastry Flour	500 mL
1 tbsp	baking powder	15 mL
¾ tsp	salt	3 mL
1⅓ cups	butter, softened	325 mL
1⅓ cups	granulated sugar	325 mL
1½ tsp	vanilla	7 mL
4	eggs	4
½ cup	milk	125 mL
¼ cup	poppy seeds	50 mL

Filling

2	eggs	2
2 tbsp	grated lemon zest	30 mL
6 tbsp	fresh lemon juice	90 mL
1 cup	granulated sugar	250 mL
¼ cup	butter, softened	50 mL

Frosting

½ cup	butter, softened	125 mL
4 cups	confectioner's (icing) sugar, sifted	1 L
1 tbsp	grated lemon zest	15 mL
2 tbsp	fresh lemon juice	30 mL
¼ cup	light (10%) cream	50 mL

MAKES ABOUT 12 SERVINGS

TIPS: Use shortening, not butter or oil, to grease pans. Cooking spray works well, too.

Prepare entire cake a day ahead to let flavors mellow.

1. Cake: Combine flour, baking powder and salt. Cream butter in large bowl on medium speed of electric mixer until creamy. Gradually add sugar and vanilla, beating until light and fluffy. Add eggs, one at a time, beating well after each addition. Add dry ingredients alternately with milk, mixing lightly just to blend. Fold in poppy seeds. (Batter will be quite stiff.) Spread batter evenly in prepared pans. Bake for 35 to 40 minutes or until toothpick inserted in center comes out clean. Cool for 10 minutes, then remove from pans and cool completely.

2. Filling: Beat together eggs, lemon zest, juice and sugar in small saucepan. Add butter. Cook over low heat, stirring constantly, until thickened. Cool completely. Mixture will thicken on cooling. Prepare several days ahead, if desired. Refrigerate until using.

3. Frosting: Beat together all ingredients until smooth and creamy.

4. Assembly: Cut cake layers in half horizontally to make four layers. Place one layer on serving plate. Spread half of the filling on top. Place second cake layer over filling and spread with some of the frosting. Top with another cake layer, remaining filling and last cake layer. Cover sides and top of cake with remaining frosting.

VARIATION: The amount of poppy seeds used is a matter of personal taste.

Preparation time: 40 minutes / Baking time: 40 minutes / Freezing: excellent

Cherry Almond Coffee Cake

An easy-to-make cake for dessert or a coffee-time treat.

PREHEAT OVEN TO 350°F (180°C)
8½-INCH (21 CM) OR 9-INCH (23 CM) SPRINGFORM PAN, GREASED

2¼ cups	Robin Hood All-Purpose Flour	550 mL
¾ cup	granulated sugar	175 mL
¾ cup	butter or margarine	175 mL
½ tsp	baking powder	2 mL
½ tsp	baking soda	2 mL
1	egg	1
¾ cup	buttermilk or soured milk	175 mL
1 tsp	almond extract	5 mL
1	can (19 oz/540 mL) cherry pie filling	1
⅓ cup	sliced almonds	75 mL

MAKES ABOUT
8 SERVINGS

TIP: Always put a piece of aluminum foil under springform pans while baking. Often they can leak a little, so this will keep your oven clean.

1. Combine flour and sugar in large bowl. Cut in butter with pastry blender until mixture is crumbly. Set aside ½ cup (125 mL) for topping. Add baking powder and baking soda to remainder. Beat together egg, buttermilk and almond extract. Add to dry ingredients, stirring just until moistened.

2. Spread two-thirds of the batter over bottom and partway up side of prepared pan. Spoon pie filling evenly over batter. Drop small spoonfuls of remaining batter over filling. Stir almonds into reserved crumbled mixture. Sprinkle over batter.

3. Bake for 65 to 75 minutes for 8½-inch (21 cm) pan or 50 to 60 minutes for 9-inch (23 cm) pan or until toothpick inserted in center comes out clean. Cover with foil if top is becoming too brown.

VARIATION: Try apple, mixed berry or blueberry pie filling for another new taste.

Preparation time: 15 minutes /
Baking time: 1 hour or 1 hour 15 minutes /
Freezing: excellent

Company Cheesecake

*La crème de la crème of indulgence
to serve with your favorite berry sauce.*

PREHEAT OVEN TO 400°F (200°C) • 10-INCH (25 CM) SPRINGFORM PAN

Crust

2 cups	Robin Hood All-Purpose Flour	500 mL
½ cup	granulated sugar	125 mL
2 tsp	grated lemon zest	10 mL
1 cup	butter or margarine	250 mL
1	egg, beaten	1

Filling

5	pkgs (each 8 oz/250 g) cream cheese, softened	5
1¾ cups	granulated sugar	425 mL
3 tbsp	Robin Hood All-Purpose Flour	45 mL
2 tsp	grated lemon zest	10 mL
½ tsp	vanilla	2 mL
5	eggs	5
¼ cup	whipping (35%) cream	50 mL
	Fruit pie filling or fruit sauce	

MAKES ABOUT
16 SERVINGS

TIPS: Run knife around pan rim to loosen edge of cheesecake from pan as soon as it comes out of the oven.

Serve cake at room temperature for optimum texture and flavor.

1. Crust: Combine flour, sugar, lemon zest and butter in food processor or mixing bowl until crumbly. Add egg, mixing until dough forms. Remove ring from springform pan. With floured fingers, press one-third of the dough on pan bottom. Bake at 400°F (200°C) for 8 to 10 minutes or until golden. Cool. Return ring to pan. Pat remaining dough onto sides, at least 2 inches (5 cm) high.

2. Filling: Beat cream cheese in large bowl with electric mixer until smooth. Beat in sugar, flour, lemon zest and vanilla on high speed. Add eggs, one at a time, then cream, beating until smooth and light. Pour into prepared crust.

3. Place pan on baking sheet or piece of foil (grease will leak out slightly from crust). Bake at 425°F (220°C) for 12 minutes, then reduce heat to 300°F (150°C) and bake for 1 hour longer or until softly set. Cool completely. Refrigerate for 3 hours or overnight. Serve with fruit filling or sauce.

**Preparation time: 40 minutes / Baking time: 1 hour 22 minutes /
Refrigeration time: 3 hours or overnight / Freezing: excellent**

Orange Cake

A real family favorite. The fabulous flavors and texture come from grinding the whole orange with raisins and nuts.

PREHEAT OVEN TO 350°F (180°C) • 13- BY 9-INCH (3.5 L) CAKE PAN, GREASED

Cake

1	large orange	1	
1 cup	raisins	250 mL	
½ cup	walnuts	125 mL	
2 cups	Robin Hood All-Purpose Flour or 2¼ cups (550 mL) Robin Hood Best For Cake & Pastry Flour	500 mL	
1 cup	granulated sugar	250 mL	
1 tsp	baking soda	5 mL	
1 tsp	salt	5 mL	
1 cup	milk	250 mL	
½ cup	shortening	125 mL	
2	eggs	2	

Frosting

½ cup	butter, softened	125 mL
3 cups	confectioner's (icing) sugar, sifted	750 mL
1 tbsp	grated orange zest	15 mL
⅓ cup	orange juice	75 mL

MAKES ABOUT 12 SERVINGS

TIP: Submerging an orange in hot water for 15 minutes before squeezing will yield almost twice the amount of juice.

1. **Cake:** Squeeze orange; reserve juice for frosting. Grind together or finely chop in food processor orange rind and pulp, raisins and nuts. Set aside. Combine remaining cake ingredients in large mixer bowl. Beat on low speed just until blended, then on medium speed for 3 minutes. Stir in orange raisin mixture. Spread batter evenly in prepared pan. Bake for 35 to 40 minutes. Cool completely.

2. **Frosting:** Beat together all ingredients until smooth and creamy. Spread over cake.

VARIATION: Use dates in place of raisins.

Preparation time: 25 minutes / Baking time: 40 minutes / Freezing: excellent

Toffee Apple Cake

No need for a frosting — the topping bakes right on the cake.

PREHEAT OVEN TO 350°F (180°C) • 13- BY 9-INCH (3.5 L) CAKE PAN, GREASED

Cake

½ cup	butter, softened	125 mL
1 cup	granulated sugar	250 mL
2	eggs	2
1 tsp	vanilla	5 mL
2 cups	Robin Hood All-Purpose Flour	500 mL
1 tsp	baking powder	5 mL
1 tsp	baking soda	5 mL
¼ tsp	salt	1 mL
1 cup	sour cream	250 mL
2 cups	diced peeled apples	500 mL
¾ cup	toffee bits	175 mL

Topping

⅓ cup	Robin Hood All-Purpose Flour	75 mL
2 tbsp	packed brown sugar	30 mL
¼ cup	butter	50 mL
¾ cup	toffee bits	175 mL

MAKES ABOUT
15 SERVINGS

TIPS: An ideal cake for lunch boxes. Wrap individual pieces and freeze, then pack them when making lunches in the morning. They will be perfectly thawed by noon.

Toffee bits are sold in packages like chocolate chips.

1. Cake: Cream butter, sugar, eggs and vanilla in large bowl on medium speed of electric mixer until light and fluffy. Combine flour, baking powder, baking soda and salt. Add to creamed mixture alternately with sour cream, making three additions of dry ingredients and two of sour cream. Fold in apples and toffee bits. Spread batter evenly in prepared pan.

2. Topping: Combine all ingredients, mixing until crumbly. Sprinkle evenly over batter.

3. Bake for 35 to 40 minutes or until toothpick inserted in center comes out clean.

Preparation time: 20 minutes / Baking time: 40 minutes / Freezing: excellent

Crunchy Top Banana Cake

Cut into small squares, these "banana bites" make a terrific after-school treat.

PREHEAT OVEN TO 350°F (180°C) • 13- BY 9-INCH (3.5 L) CAKE PAN, GREASED

Cake

2 cups	Robin Hood All-Purpose Flour or 2¼ cups (550 mL) Robin Hood Best For Cake & Pastry Flour	500 mL
1½ tsp	baking powder	7 mL
1 tsp	baking soda	5 mL
½ tsp	salt	2 mL
1½ cups	granulated sugar	375 mL
½ cup	shortening	125 mL
¼ cup	buttermilk or soured milk	50 mL
1 cup	mashed ripe bananas (3 to 4 bananas)	250 mL
2	eggs	2
1 tsp	vanilla	5 mL
¼ cup	buttermilk or soured milk	50 mL

Topping

⅓ cup	butter	75 mL
¾ cup	packed brown sugar	175 mL
3 tbsp	light (10%) cream	45 mL
1 cup	flaked coconut	250 mL
¾ cup	chopped nuts	175 mL

MAKES ABOUT 20 SERVINGS

TIP: Watch topping closely when broiling. It will burn very quickly.

1. Cake: Combine flour, baking powder, baking soda and salt in large bowl. Add sugar, shortening, ¼ cup (50 mL) buttermilk and bananas. Beat on medium speed of electric mixer for 2 minutes. Add eggs, vanilla and ¼ cup (50 mL) buttermilk. Beat on medium speed for 1 minute. Spread batter evenly in prepared pan. Bake for 30 to 40 minutes or until toothpick inserted in center comes out clean.

2. Topping: While cake is baking, prepare topping. Melt butter in small saucepan. Stir in remaining ingredients thoroughly. Remove cake from oven and immediately spread topping evenly over cake. Broil 6 inches (15 cm) below element for 2 to 3 minutes or until bubbly and golden.

Preparation time: 15 minutes /
Baking time: 43 minutes / Freezing: excellent

Apricot Walnut Torte

"Heaven in a nutshell" perfectly describes this melt-in-your-mouth dessert.

PREHEAT OVEN TO 350°F (180°C)
TWO 8-INCH (1.2 L) ROUND CAKE PANS, GREASED AND FLOURED

Cake

¾ cup	Robin Hood All-Purpose or Best For Cake & Pastry Flour	175 mL
2 tsp	baking powder	10 mL
½ tsp	salt	2 mL
1 cup	ground walnuts	250 mL
4	egg yolks	4
2 tbsp	water	30 mL
1 tsp	vanilla	5 mL
¾ cup	granulated sugar	175 mL
4	egg whites	4
¼ cup	granulated sugar	50 mL

Filling & Glaze

2 cups	whipping (35%) cream	500 mL
¼ cup	confectioner's (icing) sugar, sifted	50 mL
1	jar (7½ oz/213 mL) junior apricots (baby food)	1
½ cup	strained apricot jam	125 mL
2 tbsp	chopped walnuts, optional	30 mL

MAKES ABOUT 8 SERVINGS

TIP: Prepare cakes ahead and freeze. Assemble when the need arises.

1. **Cake:** Combine flour, baking powder, salt and nuts in mixing bowl. Beat egg yolks, water and vanilla in small bowl on high speed of electric mixer until thick and light. Gradually add ¾ cup (175 mL) sugar, beating until thick and light, about 5 minutes. Beat egg whites and ¼ cup (50 mL) sugar to stiff peaks. Fold dry ingredients into egg yolk mixture in four portions. Gently fold in meringue. Spread batter evenly in prepared pans. Bake for 25 to 30 minutes or until toothpick inserted in center comes out clean. Cool in pans for 5 minutes, then remove and cool completely on wire rack.

2. **Filling & Glaze:** Beat cream and confectioner's sugar to stiff peaks. Fold in apricots. Cut cake layers in half horizontally. Fill layers with apricot cream filling. Glaze top with apricot jam. Garnish with chopped walnuts, if desired. Refrigerate until serving.

VARIATION: Substitute pecans or hazelnuts for walnuts.

Preparation time: 40 minutes / Baking time: 30 minutes / Freezing: excellent, plain cake layers

Lemon Almond Cake

A light and refreshing cake that needs no frosting.

PREHEAT OVEN TO 350°F (180°C)
10-INCH (3 L) BUNDT OR 10-INCH (4 L) TUBE PAN, GREASED AND FLOURED

Cake

3 cups	Robin Hood All-Purpose Flour	750 mL
1 tbsp	baking powder	15 mL
1 tsp	salt	5 mL
¾ cup	butter, softened	175 mL
2 cups	granulated sugar	500 mL
4	eggs	4
1 cup	milk	250 mL
2 tbsp	grated lemon zest	30 mL
1 cup	ground almonds	250 mL

Glaze

¾ cup	granulated sugar	175 mL
⅓ cup	lemon juice	75 mL

MAKES ABOUT
12 SERVINGS

TIP: A nice cake to prepare a day ahead, allowing the glaze to soak into the cake.

1. Cake: Combine flour, baking powder and salt. Cream butter and sugar in large bowl on medium speed of electric mixer until light. Add eggs, one at a time, beating until light and fluffy. On low speed, add dry ingredients to creamed mixture alternately with milk, mixing lightly after each addition. Stir in lemon zest and almonds.

2. Spread batter evenly in prepared pan. Bake for 60 to 65 minutes or until toothpick inserted in center comes out clean. Cool in pan for 20 minutes. Remove from pan and place on cake plate.

3. Glaze: Heat sugar and lemon juice together in small saucepan until sugar is dissolved. Prick surface of cake with fork, toothpick or skewer. Brush warm cake with glaze. Repeat brushing until all glaze is used.

Preparation time: 15 minutes / Baking time: 1 hour 5 minutes / Freezing: excellent

Old-Fashioned Raisin Spice Cake

A moist, spicy everyday cake that freezes well.

PREHEAT OVEN TO 375°F (190°C)
9-INCH (2.5 L) SQUARE CAKE PAN, GREASED

Cake

2	egg whites	2
1⅓ cups	Robin Hood All-Purpose Flour or 1½ cups (375 mL) Robin Hood Best For Cake & Pastry Flour	325 mL
1½ tsp	baking powder	7 mL
½ tsp	salt	2 mL
2 tsp	cinnamon	10 mL
1 tsp	ground allspice	5 mL
½ tsp	ground cloves	2 mL
½ cup	butter or margarine, softened	125 mL
1 cup	granulated sugar	250 mL
2	egg yolks	2
⅔ cup	milk	150 mL
1 tsp	vanilla	5 mL
¾ cup	raisins	175 mL

Frosting

¼ cup	butter or margarine, softened	50 mL
2 cups	confectioner's (icing) sugar, sifted	500 mL
1 tbsp	lemon juice	15 mL
1 to 2 tbsp	cream or milk	15 to 30 mL
	Chopped walnuts, optional	

MAKES ABOUT
12 SERVINGS

TIP: Do not use a plastic bowl when beating egg whites since oils retained in the plastic prevent the egg whites from forming stiff peaks. Be sure the beaters are clean and dry.

1. Cake: Beat egg whites to stiff but moist peaks. Combine flour, baking powder, salt and spices in large bowl. Stir well to blend. Add butter, sugar, egg yolks, milk and vanilla. Beat on low speed of electric mixer for 30 seconds to blend, then on medium speed until smooth, about 1½ minutes. Stir in raisins. Fold in stiff egg whites. Spread batter evenly in prepared pan. Bake for 30 to 35 minutes. Cool completely.

2. Frosting: Cream together butter, half of the confectioner's sugar and lemon juice until light. Gradually add remaining confectioner's sugar and enough cream to make a smooth, spreadable consistency. Spread over cooled cake. Sprinkle with walnuts, if desired.

VARIATION: Adjust spices to suit your own personal taste.

Preparation time: 15 minutes / Baking time: 35 minutes / Freezing: excellent

Triple Chocolate Fudge Cake

How can you go wrong with a combination of chocolate cake, filling and glaze?

PREHEAT OVEN TO 350°F (180°C)
TWO 9-INCH (1.5 L) ROUND CAKE PANS, GREASED AND FLOURED

Cake

2¼ cups	Robin Hood Best For Cake & Pastry Flour or 2 cups (500 mL) Robin Hood All-Purpose Flour	550 mL
2 tsp	baking soda	10 mL
½ tsp	salt	2 mL
½ cup	butter, softened	125 mL
2¼ cups	packed brown sugar	550 mL
3	eggs	3
1½ tsp	vanilla	7 mL
3	squares (each 1 oz/28 g) unsweetened chocolate, melted and cooled	3
1 cup	sour cream	250 mL
1 cup	boiling water	250 mL

Filling

½ cup	butter, softened	125 mL
3 to 3½ cups	confectioner's (icing) sugar, sifted	750 to 875 mL
⅓ cup	light (10%) cream	75 mL
2	squares (each 1 oz/28 g) unsweetened chocolate, melted and cooled	2

Glaze

4	squares (each 1 oz/28 g) unsweetened chocolate	4
2 tbsp	strong brewed coffee	30 mL
3 tbsp	butter, softened	45 mL

MAKES ABOUT 12 SERVINGS

TIP: Don't be surprised that the batter is quite thin.

1. Cake: Combine flour, baking soda and salt. Beat butter, sugar and eggs on medium speed of electric mixer until light, about 5 minutes. Beat in vanilla and melted chocolate. Add dry ingredients alternately with sour cream, mixing lightly until smooth. Stir in boiling water. (Batter will be thin.) Pour into prepared pans. Bake for 30 to 35 minutes or until toothpick inserted in center comes out clean. Cool for 10 minutes, then remove from pans and cool completely.

2. Filling: Beat together all ingredients with electric mixer until light and fluffy. If necessary, add a little more confectioner's sugar or cream to make a spreadable consistency. Spread some of the filling between cake layers. Spread sides of cake with remaining filling. Refrigerate for 30 minutes.

3. Glaze: Melt chocolate in coffee over low heat, stirring until smooth. Remove from heat. Gradually add butter, blending until smooth. Spread glaze over top of cake, letting it drizzle down sides. Let glaze set before cutting.

VARIATION: Omit coffee in the glaze, if desired.

**Preparation time: 30 minutes / Baking time: 35 minutes /
Refrigeration time: 30 minutes / Freezing: excellent**

Character Cupcakes

Let your kids shine making yummy face cupcakes.

PREHEAT OVEN TO 350°F (180°C) • 24-CUP MUFFIN PAN, PAPER-LINED

Cupcakes

3 cups	Robin Hood All-Purpose Flour or 3⅓ cups (825 mL) Robin Hood Best For Cake & Pastry Flour	750 mL
2 cups	granulated sugar	500 mL
2 tsp	baking soda	10 mL
1 tsp	salt	5 mL
2 cups	water	500 mL
¾ cup	vegetable oil	175 mL
3	squares (each 1 oz/28 g) unsweetened chocolate, melted and cooled	3
2 tsp	vinegar	10 mL
2 tsp	vanilla	10 mL

Decoration

2 cups	chocolate or vanilla frosting	500 mL
	Candies, nuts, gumdrops, licorice, jelly beans, marshmallows, etc.	

MAKES 2 DOZEN
CUPCAKES

TIPS: Use lemon juice in place of vinegar in batter, if desired.

There's no egg in the recipe — a good choice if there are egg allergies in the family.

1. Cupcakes: Combine flour, sugar, baking soda and salt in large bowl. Add water, oil, melted chocolate, vinegar and vanilla. Beat on medium speed of electric mixer for 30 seconds or with wooden spoon for 1 minute or just until smooth. Spoon batter into muffin cups. Bake for 15 to 20 minutes or until toothpick inserted in center comes out clean. Remove from pan. Cool completely.

2. Decoration: Spread about 1½ tbsp (20 mL) of the frosting on top of each cupcake. Use your favorite colorful candies and your creativity to make characters.

Decoration time: All day! / Baking time: 20 minutes / Freezing: excellent, undecorated

Tropical Treat Cake

Several fruits combine in a wonderfully moist cake that needs no frosting. It's a nice snack or lunch-box cake or a pleasing dessert served with a dollop of whipped cream.

PREHEAT OVEN TO 350°F (180°C)
9-INCH (2.5 L) SQUARE CAKE PAN, GREASED

1	large orange	1
1	medium banana	1
1 cup	raisins	250 mL
1¾ cups	Robin Hood All-Purpose Flour	425 mL
1 tsp	baking soda	5 mL
½ tsp	cinnamon	2 mL
¼ tsp	salt	1 mL
½ cup	shortening	125 mL
1 cup	granulated sugar	250 mL
2	eggs	2
½ cup	buttermilk or soured milk	125 mL
1 tsp	vanilla	5 mL

MAKES ABOUT
8 SERVINGS

TIP: Use a ripe banana for the best flavor.

1. Peel and cut orange into pieces; remove seeds. Combine orange, banana and raisins in food processor and chop coarsely. Combine flour, baking soda, cinnamon and salt.

2. Cream together shortening, sugar and eggs in large bowl on high speed of electric mixer until light and creamy. Add fruit mixture. Add dry ingredients alternately with buttermilk and vanilla, mixing lightly after each addition. Spread batter evenly in prepared pan. Bake for 50 to 55 minutes or until toothpick inserted in center comes out clean.

Preparation time: 15 minutes / Baking time: 55 minutes / Freezing: excellent

Sunny Citrus Pound Cake

Plain and simple is often the most delicious. Serve unadorned with coffee for an afternoon treat or as dessert with fresh fruit.

PREHEAT OVEN TO 350°F (180°C)
10-INCH (3 L) BUNDT OR 10-INCH (4 L) TUBE PAN, GREASED AND FLOURED

Cake

3 cups	Robin Hood All-Purpose Flour	750 mL	
¾ tsp	salt	3 mL	
½ tsp	baking powder	2 mL	
½ tsp	baking soda	2 mL	
1 cup	unsalted butter, softened	250 mL	
2¼ cups	granulated sugar	550 mL	
4	eggs	4	
1 tbsp	grated orange zest	15 mL	
2 tsp	grated lemon zest	10 mL	
¾ cup	plain yogurt	175 mL	
⅓ cup	orange juice	75 mL	

Glaze (optional)

⅓ cup	granulated sugar	75 mL
¼ cup	lemon juice	50 mL

MAKES ABOUT
16 SERVINGS

TIP: Expect a crack on top. This is typical of most pound cakes.

1. Cake: Combine flour, salt, baking powder and baking soda; set aside. Cream butter and sugar in large mixer bowl on medium speed of electric mixer until well blended. Add eggs, one at a time, beating lightly after each until smooth, then beat on high speed until thick and creamy, about 5 minutes. Add zests. Add dry ingredients alternately with yogurt and orange juice, beating on low speed until blended. Spread batter in prepared pan. Bake for 65 to 75 minutes or until toothpick inserted in center comes out clean. Cool for 10 minutes in pan, then remove to wire rack.

2. Glaze: Heat together sugar and juice, stirring to dissolve sugar. Poke holes with toothpick, skewer or fork in surface of warm cake. Brush glaze over cake, letting it soak in. Cool cake completely before slicing.

VARIATION: For an orange cake, omit lemon zest in cake and use orange juice in the glaze.

Preparation time: 25 minutes / Baking time: 1 hour 15 minutes / Freezing: excellent, not glazed

Moist and Chewy Caramel Apple Cake

An ideal company or family dessert. Nuts and coconut on top are covered with a caramel topping that soaks into the cake for a great finish.

PREHEAT OVEN TO 350°F (180°C) • 13- BY 9-INCH (3.5 L) CAKE PAN, GREASED

2½ cups	Robin Hood All-Purpose Flour	625 mL	**MAKES ABOUT 12 SERVINGS**
2 cups	granulated sugar	500 mL	
2 tsp	salt	10 mL	
1½ tsp	baking soda	7 mL	**TIP:** Flaked coconut is best. The shredded variety seems a bit too stringy.
½ tsp	baking powder	2 mL	
½ cup	undiluted evaporated milk	125 mL	
⅓ cup	water	75 mL	
2	eggs, lightly beaten	2	
2 cups	chopped peeled apples	500 mL	
⅓ cup	packed brown sugar	75 mL	
1 cup	flaked coconut	250 mL	
½ cup	chopped nuts	125 mL	
¾ cup	undiluted evaporated milk	175 mL	
20	individual vanilla caramels	20	

1. Combine flour, sugar, salt, baking soda and baking powder in large bowl. Combine ½ cup (125 mL) evaporated milk, water, eggs and apples in medium bowl. Stir into dry ingredients. Mix well. Spread batter evenly in prepared pan. Sprinkle with brown sugar, then coconut and nuts. Bake for 40 to 45 minutes or until top springs back when lightly touched. Cover loosely with foil if topping is becoming too brown.

2. Meanwhile, combine ¾ cup (175 mL) evaporated milk and caramels in small saucepan. Cook, stirring, over low heat until mixture is smooth. Pour evenly over hot cake. Cool completely before serving.

VARIATION: Pecans, walnuts and almonds all work well.

Preparation time: 20 minutes / Baking time: 45 minutes / Freezing: excellent

Cranberry Kuchen

This cranberry kuchen is a moist and delicious coffee cake.

PREHEAT OVEN TO 350°F (180°C)
10-INCH (25 CM) SPRINGFORM PAN, GREASED

Cake

½ cup	butter or margarine	125 mL
1 cup	granulated sugar	250 mL
1 tsp	vanilla	5 mL
3	eggs	3
2 cups	Robin Hood All-Purpose Flour or 2¼ cups (550 mL) Robin Hood Best For Cake & Pastry Flour	500 mL
2 tsp	baking powder	10 mL
½ tsp	baking soda	2 mL
½ tsp	salt	2 mL
1¼ cups	sour cream	300 mL
2 cups	chopped cranberries	500 mL
¼ cup	granulated sugar	50 mL

Topping

¼ cup	packed brown sugar	50 mL
2 tbsp	Robin Hood All-Purpose or Best For Cake & Pastry Flour	30 mL
2 tbsp	chopped almonds	30 mL
1 tbsp	butter or margarine, softened	15 mL
½ tsp	cinnamon	2 mL

MAKES ABOUT
12 SERVINGS

TIP: Too little greasing or leaving cakes in pans too long can cause sticking. To prevent sticking, grease pans generously with shortening (not butter or oil) and remove cake after cooling for 10 minutes.

1. **Cake:** Cream together butter, 1 cup (250 mL) sugar and vanilla in large bowl with electric mixer. Add eggs, one at a time, beating until light and fluffy. Combine flour, baking powder, baking soda and salt. Alternately add dry ingredients and sour cream to creamed mixture, ending with dry ingredients. (Batter will be fairly thick.) Combine cranberries and ¼ cup (50 mL) sugar. Spread half of the batter in prepared pan and sprinkle with cranberry mixture. Top with remaining batter.

2. **Topping:** Combine all ingredients; sprinkle over batter. Bake for 50 to 55 minutes or until toothpick inserted in center comes out clean.

VARIATION: Add 1 tbsp (15 mL) grated orange zest to batter.

Preparation time: 20 minutes / Baking time: 55 minutes / Freezing: excellent

Bars and Squares

Butterscotch Nut Bars

Try warm with ice cream for dessert.

PREHEAT OVEN TO 350°F (180°C) • 13- BY 9-INCH (3.5 L) CAKE PAN, GREASED

Crust

2 cups	Robin Hood All-Purpose Flour	500 mL
½ cup	granulated sugar	125 mL
¾ cup	butter or margarine	175 mL

Topping

4	eggs	4
1 cup	granulated sugar	250 mL
1 cup	corn syrup	250 mL
¼ cup	butter or margarine, melted	50 mL
1¾ cups	butterscotch chips	425 mL
1⅓ cups	coarsely chopped pecans	325 mL

MAKES ABOUT
2 DOZEN BARS

TIP: Store nuts in the freezer to keep fresh.

1. Crust: Combine all ingredients, mixing until crumbly. Press firmly into prepared pan. Bake for 15 to 18 minutes or until light golden.
2. Topping: Beat together eggs, sugar, corn syrup and butter until blended. Stir in butterscotch chips and pecans. Pour evenly over crust. Bake for about 30 minutes longer or until set and golden. Cool completely, then cut into bars.

VARIATION: Walnuts, almonds and hazelnuts are a good choice, too.

Preparation time: 20 minutes / Baking time: 48 minutes / Freezing: excellent

Chocolate and Almond Caramel Bars

A chewy caramel bar filled with creamy white chocolate and crunchy almonds on an oatmeal crust.

PREHEAT OVEN TO 350°F (180°C) • 13- BY 9-INCH (3.5 L) CAKE PAN, GREASED

Crust

2 cups	Robin Hood All-Purpose Flour	500 mL
2 cups	Robin Hood or Old Mill Oats	500 mL
1 cup	packed brown sugar	250 mL
1 tsp	baking soda	5 mL
1 cup	butter or margarine, melted	250 mL

Topping

1½ cups	white chocolate chips	375 mL
1 cup	slivered almonds	250 mL
1 cup	toffee bits	250 mL
1⅓ cups	caramel sundae sauce	325 mL
⅓ cup	Robin Hood All-Purpose Flour	75 mL

MAKES ABOUT
5 DOZEN BARS

TIP: These bars are delicious but rich. Cut into small pieces.

1. Crust: Combine first four ingredients in mixing bowl. Add melted butter. Mix well. Reserve 1 cup (250 mL) of the mixture for topping. Press remainder into prepared cake pan. Bake for 12 to 15 minutes or until light golden.

2. Topping: Combine chocolate chips, almonds and toffee bits. Sprinkle evenly over base. Mix together sundae sauce and flour until smooth. Pour evenly over crust. Sprinkle reserved oat mixture on top. Bake for 20 to 25 minutes longer or until golden. Cool completely, then cut into bars.

Preparation time: 15 minutes / Baking time: 40 minutes / Freezing: excellent

Chocolate Peanut Butter Oat Bars

Swirls of chocolate and creamy peanut butter top a chewy oat cookie base.

PREHEAT OVEN TO 350°F (180°C)
8-INCH (2 L) OR 9-INCH (2.5 L) SQUARE CAKE PAN, GREASED

½ cup	butter or margarine, softened	125 mL
½ cup	packed brown sugar	125 mL
½ cup	corn syrup	125 mL
1 tsp	vanilla	5 mL
3 cups	Robin Hood or Old Mill Oats	750 mL
½ cup	semi-sweet chocolate chips	125 mL
¼ cup	creamy peanut butter	50 mL

MAKES ABOUT
2 DOZEN BARS

TIP: Swirl topping gently for a more attractive look.

1. Cream butter, brown sugar, corn syrup and vanilla in large bowl on medium speed of electric mixer until smooth. Stir in oats, mixing thoroughly. Press firmly into prepared pan. Bake for 25 to 30 minutes or until light golden and center is barely firm. Cool for 5 minutes. Sprinkle chocolate chips evenly on top. Drop small spoonfuls of peanut butter over chips. Let stand for 5 minutes to soften. Swirl chocolate and peanut butter together to marble. Cool completely, then refrigerate for 15 minutes to set topping. Cut into bars.

VARIATION: A sprinkling of chopped peanuts on top adds a nice touch.

**Preparation time: 20 minutes / Baking time: 30 minutes /
Refrigeration time: 15 minutes / Freezing: excellent**

Zucchini Raisin Bars

A hidden ingredient, zucchini, makes these bars wonderfully moist.

PREHEAT OVEN TO 350°F (180°C) • 9-INCH (2.5 L) SQUARE CAKE PAN, GREASED

Bar

¼ cup	butter or shortening	50 mL	
⅔ cup	packed brown sugar	150 mL	
1	egg	1	
1 tsp	vanilla	5 mL	
1 cup	Robin Hood All-Purpose Flour	250 mL	
1 tsp	baking soda	5 mL	
½ tsp	cinnamon	2 mL	
¼ tsp	ground cloves	1 mL	
1 cup	shredded unpeeled zucchini	250 mL	
½ cup	raisins	125 mL	

Frosting

1½ cups	confectioner's (icing) sugar, sifted	375 mL
¼ cup	butter or shortening	50 mL
¼ tsp	cinnamon	1 mL
1 to 2 tbsp	milk	15 to 30 mL

MAKES ABOUT
3 DOZEN BARS

TIP: You can use carrots when zucchini is not in season.

1. Bar: Cream butter, brown sugar, egg and vanilla in large bowl on medium speed of electric mixer until light and creamy. Add flour, baking soda and spices. Mix well. Stir in zucchini and raisins. Spread evenly in prepared pan. Bake for 25 to 30 minutes or until toothpick inserted in center comes out clean. Cool completely.

2. Frosting: Beat together all ingredients, adding enough milk to make a smooth spreadable consistency. Spread evenly over bars.

VARIATION: Replace ground cloves with ground ginger or nutmeg.

Preparation time: 20 minutes / Baking time: 30 minutes / Freezing: excellent

Caramel Pecan Bars

These look fabulous and taste even better. Bet your tasters can't eat just one!

PREHEAT OVEN TO 350°F (180°C) • 15- BY 10-INCH (2 L) JELLY ROLL PAN

Crust

1 cup	butter	250 mL
½ cup	packed brown sugar	125 mL
3 cups	Robin Hood All-Purpose Flour	750 mL
1	egg, beaten	1

Filling

3 cups	pecan halves	750 mL
¾ cup	butter	175 mL
½ cup	liquid honey	125 mL
¾ cup	packed brown sugar	175 mL
¼ cup	whipping (35%) cream	50 mL

MAKES ABOUT
50 BARS

TIP: Take time to place pecans right side up.

1. **Crust:** Combine all ingredients in food processor or with electric mixer until blended. Press evenly into pan. Bake for 15 minutes.

2. **Filling:** Spread pecans evenly over crust. In large, heavy saucepan over medium-high heat, melt butter with honey. Add brown sugar. Boil for 5 to 7 minutes, stirring constantly, until a rich caramel color. Remove from heat. Stir in whipping cream. Mix well and pour over pecans. Bake for 15 minutes longer. Cool completely, then cut into bars.

Preparation time: 15 minutes / Boiling time: 7 minutes / Baking time: 30 minutes / Freezing: excellent

Raspberry Almond Bars

The best granola bar your children will ever eat.

PREHEAT OVEN TO 350°F (180°C) • 9-INCH (2.5 L) SQUARE CAKE PAN, GREASED

1¾ cups	Robin Hood or Old Mill Oats	425 mL
1 cup	Robin Hood All-Purpose or Whole Wheat Flour	250 mL
1 cup	packed brown sugar	250 mL
1 tsp	baking powder	5 mL
¼ tsp	salt	1 mL
¾ cup	butter, melted	175 mL
¾ cup	raspberry jam	175 mL
½ cup	sliced almonds	125 mL

MAKES ABOUT
2 DOZEN BARS

TIP: These bars are also a favorite cut in bite-size pieces for your holiday gift cookie boxes.

1. Combine first five ingredients. Mix well. Stir in melted butter. Press two-thirds of the crumb mixture into prepared pan. Spread with jam. Add almonds to remaining crumb mixture and sprinkle over jam, patting down lightly. Bake for 25 to 30 minutes or until golden. Cool completely, then cut into bars.

Preparation time: 15 minutes / Baking time: 30 minutes / Freezing: excellent

Cranberry Pecan Bars

Combine sweet pecan pie with tart cranberries for an easy-to-eat, bite-size bar that's a sure winner.

PREHEAT OVEN TO 350°F (180°C) • 13- BY 9-INCH (3.5 L) CAKE PAN, GREASED

Crust

2 cups	Robin Hood All-Purpose Flour	500 mL
½ cup	granulated sugar	125 mL
¾ cup	butter or margarine	175 mL

Topping

4	eggs	4
1 cup	granulated sugar	250 mL
1 cup	corn syrup	250 mL
3 tbsp	butter or margarine, melted	45 mL
1¼ cups	coarsely chopped pecans	300 mL
¾ cup	coarsely chopped cranberries	175 mL

MAKES ABOUT
3 DOZEN BARS

TIP: Combine crust mixture in food processor.

1. Crust: Combine all ingredients until crumbly. Press firmly into prepared pan. Bake for 15 to 18 minutes or until light golden.

2. Topping: Beat together eggs, sugar, corn syrup and melted butter until blended. Stir in pecans and cranberries. Pour evenly over crust. Bake for about 40 minutes or until set and golden. Cool completely, then cut into bars.

VARIATION: Also delicious made with sweetened dried cranberries in place of fresh.

Preparation time: 25 minutes / Baking time: 58 minutes / Freezing: excellent

Chocolate Caramel Raspberry Bars

*How can you go wrong with a combination of creamy
chocolate-coated caramels and raspberry?*

PREHEAT OVEN TO 375°F (190°C)
8-INCH (2 L) OR 9-INCH (2.5 L) SQUARE CAKE PAN, GREASED

Topping

⅔ cup	Robin Hood All-Purpose Flour	150 mL
½ cup	chopped pecans	125 mL
⅓ cup	packed brown sugar	75 mL
6 tbsp	butter, softened	90 mL

Crust

1¼ cups	Robin Hood All-Purpose Flour	300 mL
½ cup	granulated sugar	125 mL
½ cup	butter	125 mL
⅓ cup	raspberry jam	75 mL
8 oz	milk chocolate–covered caramel balls	225 g

MAKES ABOUT
2 DOZEN BARS

TIP: Chocolate-covered caramel balls are sold in packages like chocolate chips.

1. Topping: Combine all ingredients, mixing until crumbly. Set aside.
2. Crust: Combine flour, sugar and butter, mixing until crumbly. Press firmly into prepared pan. Bake for 12 to 15 minutes or until light golden. Spread with jam and sprinkle chocolate caramel balls evenly on top. Sprinkle with topping. Bake for 15 to 20 minutes longer or until lightly browned. Cool completely, then cut into bars.

VARIATION: Try strawberry or apricot jam for another great taste.

Preparation time: 20 minutes / Baking time: 35 minutes / Freezing: excellent

Raisin Walnut Spice Bars

Old-time hermit cookies with a new twist.

PREHEAT OVEN TO 375°F (190°C) • THREE BAKING SHEETS, GREASED

1 cup	butter or margarine, softened	250 mL
2¼ cups	packed brown sugar	550 mL
3	eggs	3
⅓ cup	molasses	75 mL
4¼ cups	Robin Hood All-Purpose Flour	1050 mL
1½ tsp	baking powder	7 mL
1½ tsp	baking soda	7 mL
1½ tsp	cinnamon	7 mL
1 tsp	ground cloves	5 mL
1 tsp	ground nutmeg	5 mL
1 cup	raisins	250 mL
1 cup	chopped walnuts	250 mL
1	egg, lightly beaten	1

MAKES ABOUT 50 BARS

TIP: Ground spices lose their flavor if not properly stored. Keep in airtight containers in a cool place for about six months. Buy in small amounts that you're likely to use in this time span.

1. Cream butter and brown sugar in large bowl on medium speed of electric mixer until blended. Add eggs and molasses, beating until light and smooth.

2. Combine flour, baking powder, baking soda and spices. Stir into creamed mixture thoroughly. Add raisins and walnuts, stirring just to blend. (Dough will be soft.)

3. Shape dough on baking sheets into six logs (14 inches long by 1½ inches wide by ½ inch high (35 cm by 3.5 cm by 1 cm). Put two logs on each sheet (they spread during baking). Brush with egg to glaze. Bake for 12 to 17 minutes or until golden. Underbaking will give a chewier texture. Bake longer for a firmer bar. Cool completely, then slice diagonally into bars. Store in airtight container.

Preparation time: 15 minutes / Baking time: 17 minutes / Freezing: excellent

Crispy Peanut Butter Bars

A no-bake snack bar that's a perfect lunch-box or after-school treat.

13- BY 9-INCH (3.5 L) CAKE PAN, LINED WITH FOIL AND GREASED

2½ cups	crisp rice cereal	625 mL	MAKES ABOUT 3 DOZEN BARS
1¼ cups	Robin Hood or Old Mill Oats	300 mL	
1 cup	chopped mixed dried fruit (apricots, dates, raisins, apples, cranberries, etc.)	250 mL	**TIP:** Mix thoroughly so all dry ingredients are moistened. Mixture will seem a bit crumbly before pressing into pan.
1 cup	chopped peanuts	250 mL	
¾ cup	packed brown sugar	175 mL	
¾ cup	creamy peanut butter	175 mL	
¾ cup	liquid honey	175 mL	
½ cup	cocoa powder	125 mL	

1. Combine first four ingredients in large bowl. Heat brown sugar, peanut butter and honey in small saucepan over low heat, stirring until melted and smooth. Stir in cocoa powder. Pour over dry ingredients. Mix well. Press firmly into prepared pan. Refrigerate until set, about 1 hour. Remove from pan and peel off foil. Cut into bars.

VARIATION: Use a combination of fruits or one type only if you have a favorite.

Preparation time: 15 minutes / Refrigeration time: 1 hour / Freezing: excellent

Toffee Chocolate Bars

Layers of crunchy toffee bits, creamy caramel and chocolate top a crisp cookie base, making every bite a sheer delight.

PREHEAT OVEN TO 350°F (180°C) • 13- BY 9-INCH (3.5 L) CAKE PAN, GREASED

Crust

¾ cup	butter or margarine, softened	175 mL	
¾ cup	packed brown sugar	175 mL	
1½ cups	Robin Hood All-Purpose Flour	375 mL	

Filling

1	can (10 oz/300 mL) sweetened condensed milk	1	
2 tbsp	butter or margarine	30 mL	
1¾ cups	milk chocolate chips	425 mL	
1⅓ cups	toffee bits	325 mL	

MAKES ABOUT
4 DOZEN BARS

TIP: Pack brown sugar firmly in a dry measuring cup. It should hold its shape when turned out.

1. Crust: Cream all ingredients until well blended and mixture comes together. Press evenly into prepared pan. Bake for 20 to 25 minutes or until light golden. Cool on wire rack while preparing filling.

2. Filling: Heat sweetened condensed milk and butter in heavy saucepan, stirring constantly over medium heat for 5 to 10 minutes or until thickened. Spread over baked base. Bake for 12 to 15 minutes or until golden. Sprinkle chocolate chips evenly over top. Bake for 2 minutes longer or until chocolate is shiny and soft. Remove from oven. Spread chocolate evenly. Sprinkle toffee bits on top, pressing lightly into chocolate. Cool completely. If necessary, refrigerate just to set chocolate before cutting into bars. Store at room temperature.

VARIATION: Try semi-sweet or white chocolate chips for another taste sensation.

**Preparation time: 30 minutes / Cooking time: 10 minutes /
Baking time: 42 minutes / Freezing: excellent**

Citrus Almond Slices

Choose your favorite flavor — orange, lime or lemon.

PREHEAT OVEN TO 325°F (160°C) • BAKING SHEET, UNGREASED

Cookie

½ cup	butter or margarine, softened	125 mL
1 cup	granulated sugar	250 mL
1	egg	1
	Grated zest of 1 orange, lime or lemon	
1¾ cups	Robin Hood All-Purpose Flour	425 mL
2 tsp	baking powder	10 mL
¼ tsp	salt	1 mL
	Milk	
¾ cup	sliced almonds	175 mL

Frosting

1 cup	confectioner's (icing) sugar, sifted	250 mL
4 to 5 tsp	orange, lime or lemon juice	20 to 25 mL

MAKES ABOUT
80 SLICES

TIP: Also delicious without the frosting, if you prefer.

1. Cookie: Cream butter, sugar, egg and zest in large bowl on medium speed of electric mixer until light and creamy. Combine flour, baking powder and salt. Add to creamed mixture on low speed, mixing just until smooth. Divide dough into four pieces. Shape each into a roll 12 inches (30 cm) long. Place two rolls 4 inches (10 cm) apart on baking sheet. Flatten to 2½ inches (6 cm) wide. Brush with milk. Sprinkle almonds on top, pressing in lightly. Bake for 12 to 15 minutes or until edges are lightly browned. Cool completely.

2. Frosting: Mix confectioner's sugar and enough juice to make a smooth drizzling consistency. Drizzle over strips. Let frosting set. Cut on diagonal into ½-inch (1 cm) slices.

Preparation time: 25 minutes / Baking time: 15 minutes / Freezing: excellent

Chocolate Chip Walnut Bars

A decadent bar for the holiday season.

PREHEAT OVEN TO 350°F (180°C) • 9-INCH (2.5 L) SQUARE CAKE PAN, GREASED

Crust

1 cup	Robin Hood All-Purpose Flour	250 mL
¼ cup	granulated sugar	50 mL
⅓ cup	butter or margarine	75 mL

Topping

2	eggs	2
½ cup	granulated sugar	125 mL
½ cup	corn syrup	125 mL
2 tbsp	butter or margarine, melted	30 mL
1 cup	semi-sweet or white chocolate chips	250 mL
¾ cup	chopped walnuts	175 mL

MAKES ABOUT
2½ DOZEN BARS

TIP: Have eggs at room temperature for baking.

1. **Crust:** Combine all ingredients, mixing until crumbly. Press firmly into prepared cake pan. Bake for 12 to 15 minutes or until light golden.

2. **Topping:** Beat together eggs, sugar, corn syrup and melted butter until blended. Stir in chocolate chips and nuts. Pour evenly over crust. Bake for 25 to 30 minutes longer or until set and golden. Cool completely, then cut into bars.

VARIATIONS: Try pecans or almonds for a nice flavor change. Peanut butter chips and peanuts are great, too!

Preparation time: 20 minutes / Baking time: 45 minutes / Freezing: excellent

Oatmeal Sesame Sticks

Great for lunch boxes, your knapsack or a treat during a fall bicycle ride.

PREHEAT OVEN TO 375°F (190°C)
15- BY 10-INCH (2 L) JELLY ROLL PAN, GREASED

¾ cup	butter	175 mL	**MAKES ABOUT**
1½ cups	packed brown sugar	375 mL	**60 BARS**
1½ tsp	vanilla	7 mL	
2¼ cups	Robin Hood or Old Mill Oats	550 mL	**TIP:** One pan goes
¾ cup	sesame seeds	175 mL	a long way.
¾ tsp	baking powder	3 mL	

1. Melt butter in large saucepan. Stir in brown sugar and vanilla. Cook for 2 minutes or until mixture is bubbly. Remove from heat and stir in oats, sesame seeds and baking powder. Mix well. Press firmly with back of spoon into prepared pan. Bake for 7 to 10 minutes or until golden. Cool completely, then cut into bars.

VARIATION: Add a layer of melted chocolate on top for a more decadent taste.

Preparation time: 10 minutes / Baking time: 10 minutes / Freezing: excellent

Lemon Almond Strips

A lemon lover's delight. You can't go wrong with a supply in your freezer.

PREHEAT OVEN TO 350°F (180°C) • 13- BY 9-INCH (3.5 L) CAKE PAN, GREASED

Almond Crust

1¾ cups	Robin Hood All-Purpose Flour or 2 cups (500 mL) Robin Hood Best For Cake & Pastry Flour	425 mL
⅓ cup	granulated sugar	75 mL
½ cup	ground almonds	125 mL
1 cup	butter or margarine	250 mL

Lemon Filling

4	eggs	4
2 cups	granulated sugar	500 mL
⅓ cup	lemon juice	75 mL
¼ cup	Robin Hood All-Purpose or Best For Cake & Pastry Flour	50 mL
1 tsp	baking powder	5 mL
	Confectioner's (icing) sugar, optional	

MAKES ABOUT
45 STRIPS

TIP: Bars are popular items as they're really many cookies baked in one pan. They are easy to prepare and also easy to cut, wrap, store and transport.

1. **Crust:** Combine flour, sugar and ground almonds in mixing bowl. Cut in butter until mixture is crumbly. Press into prepared pan. Bake for 15 minutes or until light golden. Cool for 10 minutes.

2. **Filling:** Beat together eggs, sugar and lemon juice. Combine flour and baking powder; stir into eggs. Pour over baked crust. Bake for 25 to 30 minutes or just until set and light golden. Cool completely, then cut into bars. Sprinkle with confectioner's sugar before serving, if desired.

Preparation time: 15 minutes / Baking time: 45 minutes / Freezing: excellent

Chocolate Butterscotch Ripple Squares

Two favorites — chocolate and butterscotch — in every bite.

PREHEAT OVEN TO 350°F (180°C) • 13- BY 9-INCH (3.5 L) CAKE PAN, GREASED

1¾ cups	butterscotch chips	425 mL
1	can (10 oz/300 mL) sweetened condensed milk	1
2 tbsp	butter	30 mL
2¼ cups	packed brown sugar	550 mL
2	eggs	2
1 cup	butter, melted	250 mL
1½ tsp	vanilla	7 mL
1½ cups	Robin Hood All-Purpose Flour	375 mL
⅔ cup	Robin Hood or Old Mill Oats	150 mL
⅓ cup	cocoa powder	75 mL
1 cup	chopped walnuts	250 mL

MAKES ABOUT
3 DOZEN SQUARES

TIP: Cocoa powder can lump during storage. Sift before using for best results.

1. Heat together butterscotch chips, sweetened condensed milk and 2 tbsp (30 mL) butter over low heat, stirring constantly until melted and smooth. Set aside.

2. Mix together brown sugar, eggs, melted butter and vanilla until smooth. Stir in remaining ingredients. Mix well. Spread half in prepared pan. Spread butterscotch mixture evenly over base. Dot spoonfuls of remaining batter on top. Spread lightly with knife to cover filling. Bake for 30 to 35 minutes or until set. Cool completely, then cut into squares.

VARIATIONS: Any nuts work fine. Pecans, hazelnuts and almonds are also favorites. Try peanut butter chips and peanuts as well.

Preparation time: 20 minutes / Baking time: 35 minutes / Freezing: excellent

Coffee Chocolate Cheesecake Squares

Great for entertaining. One pan goes a long way.

PREHEAT OVEN TO 350°F (180°C) • 13- BY 9-INCH (3.5 L) CAKE PAN, GREASED

Brownie Layer

¾ cup	butter or margarine	175 mL
6	squares (each 1 oz/28 g) semi-sweet chocolate	6
1 tbsp	instant coffee granules	15 mL
2	eggs	2
¾ cup	packed brown sugar	175 mL
¾ cup	Robin Hood All-Purpose Flour	175 mL
½ tsp	baking powder	2 mL

Cheesecake Layer

1	pkg (8 oz/250 g) cream cheese, softened	1
½ cup	granulated sugar	125 mL
2	eggs	2
2 tbsp	Robin Hood All-Purpose Flour	30 mL
2 tbsp	strong brewed coffee or coffee liqueur	30 mL

Sour Cream Layer

1½ cups	sour cream	375 mL
3 tbsp	granulated sugar	45 mL
	Chocolate-covered coffee beans, optional	

MAKES ABOUT 4 DOZEN SQUARES

TIP: Don't overbake cheesecake. It should be soft-set when done or it may crack on top.

1. **Brownie Layer:** Melt butter and chocolate together in large saucepan until smooth. Stir in coffee granules. Cool. Add eggs and brown sugar. Mix well. Add flour and baking powder, mixing until smooth. Spread in prepared pan. Refrigerate for 10 minutes.

2. **Cheesecake Layer:** Beat cream cheese, sugar and eggs in large bowl on medium speed of electric mixer until creamy. Gradually add flour and coffee, beating until smooth. Spread over brownie layer. Bake for 20 to 25 minutes or until set.

3. **Sour Cream Layer:** Combine sour cream and sugar. Spread over cheese layer. Bake for 10 minutes longer. Cool completely, then cut into small squares. Decorate with coffee bean, if desired.

VARIATION: Bittersweet chocolate is interchangeable with semi-sweet.

Preparation time: 30 minutes / Refrigeration time: 10 minutes / Baking time: 35 minutes / Freezing: excellent

Key Lime Cheesecake Squares

A pleasant combination of tart and tangy but light and creamy. Garnish with a colorful touch of fresh fruit, if desired.

PREHEAT OVEN TO 350°F (180°C) • 8-INCH (2 L) SQUARE CAKE PAN

Crust

¾ cup	Robin Hood All-Purpose Flour	175 mL
¼ cup	packed brown sugar	50 mL
¼ cup	ground almonds	50 mL
¼ cup	butter or margarine	50 mL

Filling

1	pkg (8 oz/250 g) cream cheese, softened	1
½ cup	granulated sugar	125 mL
1	egg	1
4 tsp	lime juice	20 mL
2 tsp	grated lime zest	10 mL

MAKES ABOUT
3 DOZEN SQUARES

TIP: Decorate top with a small piece of lime, halved small strawberry or maraschino cherry.

1. Crust: Combine flour, sugar and almonds in mixing bowl. Cut in butter until mixture is crumbly. Press firmly into pan. Bake for 15 minutes.

2. Filling: Beat together all ingredients in small bowl on medium speed of electric mixer until smooth and creamy. Spread evenly over baked crust. Bake for 12 to 15 minutes or until set. Cool on wire rack. Refrigerate until chilled before cutting into small squares, about 1 hour. Serve plain or decorate as desired just before serving.

VARIATION: Replace lime juice and rind with lemon.

Preparation time: 20 minutes / Baking time: 30 minutes / Refrigeration time: 1 hour / Freezing: excellent

Lemon Almond Cranberry Squares

A thick, lemony square dotted with wonderful sweetened dried cranberries.

PREHEAT OVEN TO 350°F (180°C) • 13- BY 9-INCH (3.5 L) CAKE PAN, GREASED

Crust

2 cups	Robin Hood All-Purpose Flour	500 mL
1/3 cup	confectioner's (icing) sugar, sifted	75 mL
1 cup	butter or margarine	250 mL

Topping

4	large lemons	4
7	eggs	7
2 1/4 cups	granulated sugar	550 mL
1/4 cup	butter or margarine, melted	50 mL
1/2 cup	Robin Hood All-Purpose Flour	125 mL
2 tsp	baking powder	10 mL
1 1/4 cups	ground or finely chopped almonds	300 mL
6 oz	sweetened dried cranberries (1 cup/250 mL)	170 g

MAKES ABOUT
3 DOZEN SQUARES

TIP: Sprinkle top lightly with confectioner's (icing) sugar before serving for an attractive presentation.

1. **Crust:** Combine all ingredients until crumbly. Press firmly into prepared pan. Bake for 15 to 20 minutes or until light golden.

2. **Topping:** Reduce oven temperature to 325°F (160°C). Grate zest from two lemons. Squeeze out 3/4 cup (175 mL) juice. Beat eggs and sugar until light and slightly thickened. Stir in zest, juice and remaining ingredients. Mix well. Pour over baked crust. Bake for 40 to 50 minutes or until set and golden. Cool completely, then cut into squares.

VARIATION: Replace almonds with hazelnuts.

Preparation time: 25 minutes / Baking time: 1 hour 10 minutes / Freezing: excellent

Chocolate Butterscotch Almond Crunch

A candy-like cookie that's sure to become addictive.

PREHEAT OVEN TO 350°F (180°C) • 15- BY 10-INCH (2 L) JELLY ROLL PAN

1¾ cups	Robin Hood All-Purpose Flour	425 mL	
¾ cup	granulated sugar	175 mL	
¾ cup	packed brown sugar	175 mL	
1 cup	butter or margarine, softened	250 mL	
2	egg yolks	2	
1½ tsp	vanilla	7 mL	
1¾ cups	milk chocolate chips, melted	425 mL	
1 cup	sliced almonds, toasted	250 mL	

MAKES ABOUT 100 PIECES

TIP: A jelly roll pan is a baking sheet with sides.

1. Combine flour and sugars. Mix in butter until thoroughly blended. Add egg yolks and vanilla. Mix until smooth. OR blend in food processor until mixture comes together. Press with floured fingers into pan. Bake for 13 to 18 minutes or until light golden. Cool slightly, about 20 minutes. Spread melted chocolate over base. Sprinkle nuts on top and press in lightly. Cool until chocolate sets. Cut into squares or triangles.

VARIATION: Substitute semi-sweet or white chocolate chips for milk chocolate chips.

Preparation time: 15 minutes / Baking time: 18 minutes / Freezing: excellent

Raspberry Hazelnut Squares

Three delights — shortbread, raspberry jam and hazelnuts — stack up attractively in one square.

PREHEAT OVEN TO 350°F (180°C) • 9-INCH (2.5 L) SQUARE CAKE PAN, GREASED

Crust

½ cup	butter or margarine, softened	125 mL
½ cup	confectioner's (icing) sugar, sifted	125 mL
2	egg yolks	2
1¼ cups	Robin Hood All-Purpose Flour	300 mL

Topping

⅔ cup	raspberry jam	150 mL
2	egg whites	2
Pinch	cream of tartar	Pinch
½ cup	granulated sugar	125 mL
1 cup	toasted hazelnuts, ground	250 mL
1	square (1 oz/28 g) semi-sweet chocolate	1
1 tbsp	butter or margarine	15 mL

MAKES ABOUT 25 SQUARES

TIP: Hazelnuts and filberts are the same nut. In these squares, you can also use ground pecans or almonds.

1. Crust: Cream all ingredients until smooth. Press into prepared pan. Bake for 15 minutes or until light golden.
2. Topping: Spread jam over base. Beat egg whites and cream of tartar to soft peaks. Gradually add sugar, beating until stiff peaks form. Fold in nuts. Spread over jam. Bake for 20 to 25 minutes or until lightly browned. Cool.
3. Melt together chocolate and butter. Drizzle over squares. Let chocolate set. Cut into squares.

VARIATION: Although not as pretty, apricot jam tastes delicious, too.

Preparation time: 30 minutes / Baking time: 40 minutes / Freezing: excellent

Apricot Raisin Meringue Squares

The cinnamon meringue is crumbly to cut, but this is quickly forgotten with the first taste.

PREHEAT OVEN TO 350°F (180°C) • 13- BY 9-INCH (3.5 L) CAKE PAN, GREASED

Crust

1½ cups	Robin Hood All-Purpose Flour or 1⅔ cups (400 mL) Robin Hood Best For Cake & Pastry Flour	375 mL	**MAKES ABOUT 4 DOZEN SQUARES**
2 tbsp	granulated sugar	30 mL	
¼ tsp	salt	1 mL	**TIP:** Run knife under hot water before cutting meringue.
⅓ cup	butter	75 mL	
2	egg yolks, beaten	2	
¼ cup	sour cream	50 mL	

Filling

1¼ cups	raisins	300 mL
¾ cup	sour cream	175 mL
½ cup	apricot jam	125 mL
2	egg whites	2
½ cup	granulated sugar	125 mL
½ tsp	cinnamon	2 mL
⅓ cup	finely chopped walnuts or pecans	75 mL

1. Crust: Combine flour, sugar and salt in mixing bowl. Cut in butter until crumbly. Stir in egg yolks and sour cream. Mix well. Press into prepared pan. Bake for 15 to 20 minutes or until light golden.

2. Filling: Combine raisins, sour cream and jam. Spread evenly over crust. Beat egg whites to soft peaks. Gradually add sugar and cinnamon, beating to stiff peaks. Carefully spread meringue over raisin mixture. Sprinkle with nuts. Bake for 25 to 30 minutes or until light brown. Cool completely, then cut into squares.

VARIATION: Replace apricot jam with raspberry or strawberry.

Preparation time: 20 minutes / Baking time: 50 minutes / Freezing: not recommended

Cookies

Chocolate Chunk Pecan Cookies

Don't count on these lasting very long.

PREHEAT OVEN TO 375°F (190°C) • COOKIE SHEET, UNGREASED

1 cup	butter or margarine, softened	250 mL
¾ cup	packed brown sugar	175 mL
½ cup	granulated sugar	125 mL
1	egg	1
1 tsp	vanilla	5 mL
2 cups	Robin Hood All-Purpose Flour	500 mL
1 tsp	baking soda	5 mL
¼ tsp	salt	1 mL
6	squares (each 1 oz/28 g) semi-sweet chocolate, chopped	6
¾ cup	coarsely chopped pecans	175 mL

MAKES ABOUT
3 DOZEN COOKIES

TIP: For storage, pack cookies in single layers between waxed paper in airtight container.

1. Cream first five ingredients in large bowl on medium speed of electric mixer until light and creamy.
2. Combine flour, baking soda and salt. Add to creamed mixture, beating on low speed until blended. Stir in remaining ingredients.
3. Drop dough by heaping tablespoonfuls (20 mL) about 2 inches (5 cm) apart onto prepared cookie sheet. Bake for 9 to 12 minutes or until light golden. Cool for 5 minutes on sheet, then transfer to rack and cool completely.

VARIATION: Choose your favorite nut and chocolate.

Preparation time: 15 minutes / Baking time: 12 minutes / Freezing: excellent

Oatmeal Chocolate Chip Cookies

Always a favorite with the young and the young at heart.

PREHEAT OVEN TO 350°F (180°C) • COOKIE SHEET, GREASED

¾ cup	butter or margarine, softened	175 mL	**MAKES ABOUT 3½ DOZEN COOKIES**
¾ cup	packed brown sugar	175 mL	
⅓ cup	granulated sugar	75 mL	
1	egg	1	**TIP:** Underbake for a chewy cookie. Bake longer for crisp ones.
2 tbsp	water	30 mL	
2 tsp	vanilla	10 mL	
¾ cup	Robin Hood All-Purpose or Whole Wheat Flour	175 mL	
¾ tsp	baking soda	3 mL	
2½ cups	Robin Hood or Old Mill Oats	625 mL	
1½ cups	semi-sweet chocolate chips	375 mL	

1. Cream first six ingredients in large bowl on medium speed of electric mixer until light and creamy.
2. Combine flour and baking soda. Add to creamed mixture, beating on low speed until blended. Stir in oats and chocolate chips. Drop dough by heaping tablespoonfuls (20 mL) about 2 inches (5 cm) apart onto prepared cookie sheet. Bake for 12 to 15 minutes or until light golden. Cool for 5 minutes on sheet, then transfer to rack and cool completely.

VARIATION: Replace chips with raisins.

Preparation time: 15 minutes / Baking time: 15 minutes / Freezing: excellent

Golden Molasses Gems

Crunchy on the outside, chewy on the inside, these spicy cookies will bring back memories of early childhood and Grandma's homemade treats.

PREHEAT OVEN TO 350°F (180°C) • COOKIE SHEET, GREASED

¾ cup	shortening	175 mL
1 cup	granulated sugar	250 mL
¼ cup	molasses	50 mL
1	egg	1
2 cups	Robin Hood All-Purpose Flour	500 mL
2 tsp	baking soda	10 mL
1 tsp	cinnamon	5 mL
½ tsp	ground cloves	2 mL
½ tsp	ground ginger	2 mL
¼ tsp	salt	1 mL
1 cup	raisins	250 mL
	Granulated sugar	

MAKES ABOUT 4 DOZEN COOKIES

TIP: The cookies flatten and spread during baking, forming an interesting cracked top.

1. Cream shortening and sugar in large bowl on medium speed of electric mixer until light and fluffy. Add molasses and egg. Mix well.

2. Combine flour, baking soda, spices and salt. Add to creamed mixture. Mix well. Stir in raisins. If desired, cover and refrigerate for about 1 hour for easy shaping.

3. Shape dough into 1-inch (2.5 cm) balls. Roll in sugar to coat well. Place about 2 inches (5 cm) apart on prepared cookie sheet. Bake for 10 to 14 minutes or until set. Cool for 5 minutes on sheet, then transfer to rack and cool completely.

VARIATION: Adjust the spice level to suit your own taste.

Preparation time: 20 minutes / Baking time: 14 minutes / Freezing: excellent

Butterscotch Honey Cereal Crunchies

Kids will try to convince you they love their breakfast cereal this way.

PREHEAT OVEN TO 375°F (190°C) • COOKIE SHEET, UNGREASED

2 cups	Robin Hood All-Purpose Flour	500 mL	
1 tsp	baking soda	5 mL	
½ tsp	baking powder	2 mL	
1 cup	butter or margarine, softened	250 mL	
½ cup	granulated sugar	125 mL	
½ cup	packed brown sugar	125 mL	
⅓ cup	liquid honey	75 mL	
1	egg	1	
1¾ cups	butterscotch chips	425 mL	
2 cups	cornflake cereal, slightly crushed	500 mL	
2 cups	crisp rice cereal	500 mL	
1 cup	flaked coconut, optional	250 mL	

MAKES ABOUT
6 DOZEN COOKIES

TIP: Replace baking powder and soda every six months.

1. Combine flour, baking soda and baking powder.
2. Cream butter, sugars, honey and egg thoroughly. Add dry ingredients to creamed mixture, mixing well. Stir in remaining ingredients.
3. Drop dough by tablespoonfuls (15 mL) about 2 inches (5 cm) apart onto cookie sheet. Bake for 8 to 10 minutes or until golden. Cool for 5 minutes on sheet, then transfer to rack and cool completely.

VARIATION: Replace butterscotch chips with peanut butter chips.

Preparation time: 20 minutes / Baking time: 10 minutes / Freezing: excellent

Lemon Sugar Wafers

A hint of lemon in a tender-crisp sugar cookie.

PREHEAT OVEN TO 325°F (160°C) • COOKIE SHEET, GREASED

2 cups	granulated sugar	500 mL	
1 cup	butter, softened	250 mL	
2	eggs	2	
1 tbsp	grated lemon zest	15 mL	
¼ cup	lemon juice	50 mL	
1 tsp	vanilla	5 mL	
3½ cups	Robin Hood Best For Cake & Pastry Flour	875 mL	
1 tsp	baking soda	5 mL	
1 tsp	salt	5 mL	
1 tsp	cream of tartar	5 mL	
	Granulated sugar		

MAKES ABOUT 6 DOZEN COOKIES

TIP: Store crisp cookies in container with loose-fitting lid. If cookies become soft, place in single layer on ungreased baking sheet and heat in 300°F (150°C) oven for 5 minutes.

1. Cream sugar, butter, eggs, lemon zest, juice and vanilla in large mixing bowl until smooth. Stir in flour, baking soda, salt and cream of tartar until well blended. Refrigerate for 1 hour.

2. Shape dough into 1-inch (2.5 cm) balls. Roll in sugar. Place 2 inches (5 cm) apart on prepared cookie sheet. Bake for 15 to 20 minutes or until light golden brown. Cookies will be soft in center. Cool for 5 minutes on sheet, then transfer to rack and cool completely.

Preparation time: 20 minutes / Refrigeration time: 1 hour / Baking time: 20 minutes / Freezing: excellent

Butterscotch No-Bakes

Quick to mix, these cookies taste like candy.

BAKING SHEET, LINED WITH WAXED PAPER

1½ cups	granulated sugar	375 mL
½ cup	butter or margarine	125 mL
⅔ cup	evaporated milk	150 mL
1 cup	butterscotch chips	250 mL
3½ cups	Robin Hood or Old Mill Oats	875 mL
½ cup	flaked coconut	125 mL

MAKES ABOUT 5 DOZEN COOKIES

TIP: Refrigerate cookies in airtight container.

1. Combine sugar, butter and evaporated milk in saucepan. Bring to a boil and boil for 1 minute, stirring constantly. Remove from heat and add butterscotch chips. Stir until smooth. Stir in oats and coconut. Mix thoroughly. Cool for 5 to 10 minutes. Drop by rounded teaspoonfuls (5 mL) onto waxed paper. Refrigerate until firm, about 1 hour.

Preparation time: 15 minutes / Cooking time: 1 minute / Cooling time: 10 minutes / Refrigeration time: 1 hour / Freezing: excellent

Date 'n' Nut Drops

A spicy old-fashioned favorite drop cookie that's loaded with good taste.

PREHEAT OVEN TO 375°F (190°C) • COOKIE SHEET, GREASED

2 cups	Robin Hood All-Purpose Flour	500 mL	**MAKES ABOUT 6 DOZEN COOKIES**
1 tsp	baking soda	5 mL	
1 lb	dates, chopped	500 g	**TIP:** Store chewy cookies in airtight containers.
1 cup	shortening	250 mL	
1½ cups	packed brown sugar	375 mL	
2	eggs	2	
2 tsp	vanilla	10 mL	
1 cup	Robin Hood or Old Mill Oats	250 mL	
¾ cup	flaked coconut	175 mL	
½ cup	chopped nuts	125 mL	
1¼ tsp	cinnamon	6 mL	
¼ tsp	ground nutmeg	1 mL	

1. Toss together flour, baking soda and dates to coat dates.
2. Cream shortening, brown sugar, eggs and vanilla in large bowl on medium speed of electric mixer until light and creamy. Stir in remaining ingredients along with date mixture. Mix well.
3. Drop dough by tablespoonfuls (15 mL) about 2 inches (5 cm) apart onto prepared cookie sheet. Bake for 8 to 10 minutes or until light golden. Cool for 5 minutes on sheet, then transfer to rack and cool completely.

VARIATION: Omit nuts if desired.

Preparation time: 20 minutes / Baking time: 10 minutes / Freezing: excellent

Oatmeal Jam Sandwich Cookies

An easy-to-make turnover. Fill with your favorite flavor of jam.

PREHEAT OVEN TO 350°F (180°C) • COOKIE SHEET, GREASED

¾ cup	butter, softened	175 mL
1 cup	packed brown sugar	250 mL
½ cup	granulated sugar	125 mL
1	egg	1
2 tbsp	water	30 mL
2 tsp	vanilla	10 mL
⅔ cup	Robin Hood All-Purpose or Whole Wheat Flour	150 mL
¾ tsp	baking soda	3 mL
½ tsp	cinnamon	2 mL
3 cups	Robin Hood or Old Mill Oats	750 mL
1½ cups	raspberry jam	375 mL

MAKES ABOUT
2½ DOZEN
SANDWICH COOKIES

TIPS: Filled cookies become soft and chewy with standing.

Cookies can be stored unfilled, then assembled when desired.

1. Cream butter, sugars, egg, water and vanilla in large bowl on medium speed of electric mixer until light and fluffy.

2. Combine flour, baking soda and cinnamon. Add to creamed mixture, beating on low speed until blended. Stir in oats. Drop dough by tablespoonfuls (15 mL) about 2 inches (5 cm) apart onto prepared cookie sheet. Bake for 10 to 13 minutes or until edges are golden brown. Cool for 5 minutes on sheet, then transfer to rack and cool completely.

3. Spread jam on flat side of half of the cookies. Top with another cookie to form sandwiches.

**Preparation time: 25 minutes / Baking time: 13 minutes /
Freezing: excellent filled or unfilled**

Chocolatey Chocolate Chip Cookies

The ultimate triple chocolate cookie! Warning: they're addictive, especially warm.

PREHEAT OVEN TO 375°F (190°C) • COOKIE SHEET, GREASED

1⅔ cups	Robin Hood All-Purpose Flour	400 mL
⅓ cup	cocoa powder	75 mL
1 tsp	baking soda	5 mL
½ tsp	salt	2 mL
1 cup	butter or margarine, softened	250 mL
¾ cup	packed brown sugar	175 mL
½ cup	granulated sugar	125 mL
1	egg	1
2 tsp	vanilla	10 mL
1 cup	semi-sweet chocolate chips	250 mL
1 cup	white chocolate chips	250 mL
1 cup	coarsely chopped pecans	250 mL

MAKES ABOUT
4 DOZEN COOKIES

TIP: Chocolate chips can develop a whitish coating on storage. Don't worry — it disappears with baking.

1. Stir together flour, cocoa powder, baking soda and salt. Set aside.
2. Cream butter in large bowl on medium speed of electric mixer until light. Gradually beat in sugars, egg and vanilla until smooth. Blend in dry ingredients on low speed. Mix well. Stir in chocolate chips and nuts.
3. Drop dough by tablespoonfuls (15 mL) about 2 inches (5 cm) apart on prepared cookie sheet. Bake for 8 to 10 minutes or until set. Cool for 5 minutes on sheet, then transfer to rack and cool completely.

VARIATION: Vary the kind of chips and nuts to suit your taste.

Preparation time: 20 minutes / Baking time: 10 minutes / Freezing: excellent

Toffee Almond Crunch Cookies

Chewy but crunchy — a delectable treat!

PREHEAT OVEN TO 375°F (190°C) • COOKIE SHEET, GREASED

1 cup	shortening	250 mL
¾ cup	packed brown sugar	175 mL
½ cup	granulated sugar	125 mL
1	egg	1
2 tbsp	milk	30 mL
2 tsp	vanilla	10 mL
1¾ cups	Robin Hood All-Purpose Flour	425 mL
¾ cup	Robin Hood or Old Mill Oats	175 mL
1 tsp	baking soda	5 mL
¼ tsp	salt	1 mL
4	(each 1.4 oz/39 g) crunchy toffee chocolate bars, coarsely crushed (1 cup/250 mL)	4
1 cup	slivered almonds	250 mL

MAKES ABOUT
4½ DOZEN COOKIES

TIP: We like SKOR bars, but similar bars work well, too.

1. Cream shortening, sugars, egg, milk and vanilla in large bowl on medium speed of electric mixer until light and creamy.

2. Combine flour, oats, baking soda and salt. Add to creamed mixture, beating on low speed until blended. Stir in remaining ingredients.

3. Drop dough by tablespoonfuls (15 mL) about 2 inches (5 cm) apart onto prepared cookie sheet. Bake for 8 to 12 minutes or until light golden. Cool for 5 minutes on sheet, then transfer to rack and cool completely.

Preparation time: 20 minutes / Baking time: 12 minutes / Freezing: excellent

Chocolate Caramel Pecan Cookies

Try to resist eating these while they're still warm!

PREHEAT OVEN TO 375°F (190°C)
COOKIE SHEET, LINED WITH PARCHMENT PAPER OR WELL GREASED

1 cup	butter or margarine, softened	250 mL
¾ cup	packed brown sugar	175 mL
½ cup	granulated sugar	125 mL
1	egg	1
1½ tsp	vanilla	7 mL
2 cups	Robin Hood All-Purpose Flour	500 mL
1 tsp	baking soda	5 mL
¼ tsp	salt	1 mL
6	squares (each 1 oz/28 g) semi-sweet chocolate, chopped	6
25	individual vanilla caramels, quartered	25
¾ cup	coarsely chopped pecans	175 mL

MAKES ABOUT
4 DOZEN COOKIES

TIP: The caramels will melt and tend to stick. Use parchment paper for easy removal from pan.

1. Cream butter, sugars, egg and vanilla in large bowl on medium speed of electric mixer until light and creamy.

2. Combine flour, baking soda and salt. Add to creamed mixture, beating on low speed until blended. Stir in remaining ingredients.

3. Drop dough by tablespoonfuls (15 mL) about 2 inches (5 cm) apart onto prepared cookie sheet. Bake for 8 to 12 minutes or until light golden. Cool for 5 minutes on sheet, then transfer to rack and cool completely.

VARIATIONS: Try white chocolate and almonds for another great taste. Use chocolate caramels for a more chocolatey taste.

Preparation time: 20 minutes / Baking time: 12 minutes / Freezing: excellent

Sesame Snap Wafers

Try different seeds for a new look and taste.

PREHEAT OVEN TO 350°F (180°C) • COOKIE SHEET, LINED WITH
PARCHMENT PAPER OR LIGHTLY GREASED ALUMINUM FOIL

⅔ cup	Robin Hood All-Purpose Flour	150 mL
¼ tsp	baking powder	1 mL
½ cup	butter or margarine, softened	125 mL
1 cup	packed brown sugar	250 mL
1	egg	1
1 tsp	vanilla	5 mL
1¼ cups	sesame seeds, toasted	300 mL

MAKES ABOUT
6 DOZEN COOKIES

TIPS: Store in airtight containers.

Black sesame seeds are available in Asian grocery stores.

1. Combine flour and baking powder.
2. Cream butter, sugar, egg and vanilla. Add flour mixture. Mix until combined. Stir in seeds.
3. Drop by teaspoonfuls (5 mL) about 2 inches (5 cm) apart onto prepared cookie sheet. Bake for 6 to 9 minutes or until lightly browned. Cool for 5 minutes on sheet, then transfer to rack and cool completely.

VARIATION: Try with half black sesame seeds or flaxseeds and half white sesame seeds.

Preparation time: 10 minutes / Baking time: 9 minutes / Freezing: not recommended

White Chocolate Crisps

A chewy cookie with a crunch. Chunks of chocolate make cookies look quite decadent.

PREHEAT OVEN TO 375°F (190°C) • COOKIE SHEET, GREASED

1 cup	shortening	250 mL	**MAKES ABOUT 4 DOZEN COOKIES**
¾ cup	packed brown sugar	175 mL	
½ cup	granulated sugar	125 mL	**TIP:** You can use
1	egg	1	1 cup (250 mL) white
2 tbsp	milk	30 mL	chocolate chips in
1½ tsp	vanilla	7 mL	place of the chopped
1¾ cups	Robin Hood All-Purpose Flour	425 mL	chocolate.
1 tsp	baking soda	5 mL	
½ tsp	salt	2 mL	
6	squares (each 1 oz/28 g) white chocolate, coarsely chopped	6	
1½ cups	crisp rice cereal	375 mL	

1. Cream shortening, sugars, egg, milk and vanilla in large bowl on medium speed of electric mixer until light and creamy.
2. Combine flour, baking soda and salt. Add to creamed mixture, beating at low speed until blended. Stir in chocolate and cereal. Mix well.
3. Drop dough by heaping tablespoonfuls (20 mL) about 2 inches (5 cm) apart onto prepared cookie sheet. Bake for 8 to 10 minutes or until light golden. Cool for 5 minutes on sheet, then transfer to rack and cool completely.

VARIATION: Try milk chocolate chips in place of white.

Preparation time: 15 minutes / Baking time: 10 minutes / Freezing: excellent

Ice Cream Sandwiches

Always keep a supply of these on hand for a wonderful snack.

PREHEAT OVEN TO 350°F (180°C) • COOKIE SHEET, GREASED

1¼ cups	shortening	300 mL
1 cup	granulated sugar	250 mL
⅔ cup	packed brown sugar	150 mL
1	egg	1
¼ cup	liquid honey	50 mL
¼ cup	milk	50 mL
2½ cups	Robin Hood All-Purpose Flour	625 mL
1½ cups	Robin Hood or Old Mill Oats	375 mL
1 tsp	baking soda	5 mL
½ tsp	salt	2 mL
1½ cups	flaked coconut	375 mL
1 cup	chopped nuts (walnuts, pecans or peanuts)	250 mL
	Ice cream or frozen yogurt	

MAKES ABOUT
30 SANDWICH
COOKIES OR
60 PLAIN COOKIES

TIP: Freeze sandwiches or plain cookies to fill when desired. Add chocolate chips, Smarties or other favorites to the ice cream.

1. Cream first six ingredients in large bowl on medium speed of electric mixer until light and creamy.
2. Combine flour, oats, baking soda and salt. Add to creamed mixture gradually, beating at low speed until thoroughly blended. Stir in coconut and nuts.
3. Drop dough by heaping tablespoonfuls (20 mL) about 2 inches (5 cm) apart onto prepared cookie sheet. Bake for 10 to 13 minutes or until golden. Cool for 5 minutes on sheet, then transfer to rack and cool completely.
4. Assembly: Spread one cookie with generous amount of ice cream. Top with another cookie; press down lightly. Repeat with remaining cookies and ice cream. Wrap individually and freeze.

Preparation time: 25 minutes / Baking time: 13 minutes / Freezing: excellent

Chocolate Oatmeal Funny Face Cookies

Be sure to have this recipe on hand for rainy days. It will entertain children for hours, and moms and dads will be impressed with the creative results.

PREHEAT OVEN TO 350°F (180°C) • COOKIE SHEET, GREASED

Cookie

1½ cups	Robin Hood All-Purpose Flour	375 mL	
2 tsp	baking soda	10 mL	
1 tsp	salt	5 mL	
2⅓ cups	Robin Hood or Old Mill Oats	575 mL	
1 cup	shortening	250 mL	
1½ cups	packed brown sugar	375 mL	
2	eggs	2	
1 tsp	vanilla	5 mL	
1½ cups	semi-sweet chocolate chips	375 mL	
1 cup	chopped walnuts	250 mL	

MAKES ABOUT 2 DOZEN COOKIES

TIP: Have lots of candies on hand to decorate. Some won't make it to the cookies!

Decoration

3	squares (each 1 oz/28 g) unsweetened chocolate, melted	3
2 tbsp	shortening	30 mL
2¼ cups	confectioner's (icing) sugar, sifted	550 mL
⅓ cup	milk	75 mL
	Candies, nuts, gumdrops, licorice, jelly beans, etc.	

1. Cookie: Combine flour, baking soda, salt and oats. Stir well to blend. Cream shortening, brown sugar, eggs and vanilla thoroughly. Add dry ingredients. Mix well. Stir in chocolate chips and nuts. Drop dough by ¼ cupfuls (50 mL) about 4 inches (10 cm) apart onto prepared cookie sheet. Flatten with floured hands into 3½-inch (8 cm) circles. Bake for 10 to 15 minutes or until golden. Cool for 5 minutes on sheet, then transfer to rack and cool completely.

2. Decoration: Beat together first four ingredients to make smooth, spreadable frosting. Spread on cookies and use your favorite colorful candies to make faces or any other decorations you like.

VARIATION: Replace chips with raisins.

Preparation time: 20 minutes / Baking time: 15 minutes / Freezing: excellent

Breads

Cheese 'n' Tomato Grainery Bread

A versatile dough that's delicious any way you shape it.

PREHEAT OVEN TO 375°F (190°C)
8½- BY 4½-INCH (1.5 L) LOAF PAN OR 9-INCH (2.5 L) SQUARE CAKE PAN, GREASED
BREAD MACHINE

1	egg, beaten	1	
1 cup	water	250 mL	
2 tbsp	butter or margarine	30 mL	
2 tbsp	liquid honey	30 mL	
1½ cups	Robin Hood Best For Bread Homestyle White Flour	375 mL	
1 cup	Robin Hood Best For Bread Whole Wheat Flour	250 mL	
½ cup	Robin Hood or Old Mill Oats	125 mL	
½ cup	Robin Hood Red River Cereal	125 mL	
1 tsp	salt	5 mL	
1¼ tsp	bread machine yeast	6 mL	
⅔ cup	chopped sun-dried tomatoes	150 mL	
¼ cup	grated Parmesan cheese	50 mL	

MAKES 1 LOAF OR 16 ROLLS

TIP: Sun-dried tomatoes are available packed in oil at deli counters or in bottles.

1. Add ingredients to bread machine according to manufacturer's directions. Add tomatoes and cheese at "add ingredients" signal or with other dry ingredients. Select Whole Wheat cycle for bread machine loaf; or select Dough cycle to shape and bake in conventional oven.

2. Loaf: Shape dough into three or four balls. Place in prepared loaf pan and cover with tea towel. Let rise in warm place (75° to 85°F/24° to 29°C) for about 1 hour. Bake for 25 minutes. Cover with foil if becoming too brown.

3. Rolls: Shape dough into 16 balls. Place in prepared square pan. Cover with tea towel and let rise for 30 to 40 minutes. Bake for 18 to 23 minutes.

Preparation time: 20 minutes / Rising time: 1 hour for loaf, 40 minutes for rolls / Baking time: 25 minutes for loaf, 23 minutes for rolls / Freezing: excellent

Batter Rolls

Not only tender, light and delicious but easy to make, too!

PREHEAT OVEN TO 375°F (190°C) • TWO 12-CUP MUFFIN PANS, GREASED

1 tsp	granulated sugar	5 mL	
½ cup	warm water (105° to 115°F/40° to 46°C)	125 mL	
2¼ tsp	active dry yeast (1 envelope ¼ oz/8 g)	11 mL	
1½ cups	milk	375 mL	
¼ cup	granulated sugar	50 mL	
¼ cup	shortening	50 mL	
2 tsp	salt	10 mL	
2	eggs	2	
4 cups	Robin Hood All-Purpose or Best For Bread Homestyle White Flour	1 L	

MAKES ABOUT 20 ROLLS

TIP: Dough is very elastic and sticky. Use floured fingers to shape dough.

1. Dissolve 1 tsp (5 mL) sugar in warm water in large bowl. Sprinkle in yeast. Let stand for 10 minutes, then stir well.

2. Combine milk, ¼ cup (50 mL) sugar, shortening and salt in saucepan. Heat until lukewarm and shortening is melted. Stir well. Add to yeast mixture along with eggs. Add 2¾ cups (675 mL) of the flour and beat vigorously with wooden spoon or electric mixer until smooth, about 3 minutes. Gradually stir in remaining 1½ cups (375 mL) flour. (Batter will be soft.) Cover with greased waxed paper and tea towel. Let rise in warm place (75° to 85°F/24° to 29°C) until doubled, about 1 hour.

3. Stir down dough and let stand for 10 minutes. Fill prepared muffin cups three-quarters full. Let rise until doubled, 25 to 40 minutes. Bake for 15 to 20 minutes or until golden. Turn out of pans immediately. Serve warm or cool.

VARIATION: Replace shortening with butter.

Preparation time: 25 minutes / Rising time: 1 hour 40 minutes / Baking time: 20 minutes / Freezing: excellent

Hearty Oatmeal Raisin Bread

Wonderful fresh from the oven, but delicious toasted, too.

PREHEAT OVEN TO 375°F (190°C)
TWO 9- BY 5-INCH (2 L) LOAF PANS, GREASED

2 cups	milk	500 mL	
2 cups	Robin Hood or Old Mill Oats	500 mL	
⅓ cup	molasses	75 mL	
¼ cup	packed brown sugar	50 mL	
¼ cup	shortening	50 mL	
4 tsp	salt	20 mL	
1 tsp	cinnamon	5 mL	
¼ tsp	ground nutmeg	1 mL	
2 tsp	granulated sugar	10 mL	
1 cup	warm water (105° to 115°F/40° to 46°C)	250 mL	
4½ tsp	active dry yeast (2 envelopes ¼ oz/8 g each)	22 mL	
3 cups	Robin Hood Whole Wheat or Best For Bread Whole Wheat Flour	750 mL	
3 to 3½ cups	Robin Hood All-Purpose or Best For Bread Homestyle White Flour	750 to 875 mL	
1½ cups	raisins	375 mL	

MAKES 2 LOAVES

TIP: Plump raisins in boiling water if very hard. Pat dry before using.

1. Heat milk to very hot but not boiling.
2. Combine oats, molasses, brown sugar, shortening, salt, cinnamon and nutmeg in large bowl. Pour hot milk over oat mixture. Cool to lukewarm.
3. Dissolve granulated sugar in warm water. Sprinkle in yeast. Let stand for 10 minutes, then stir well. Add yeast mixture to oats mixture. Add 2 cups (500 mL) of the whole wheat flour, beating vigorously until well mixed. Stir in remaining 1 cup (250 mL) whole wheat flour and enough of the white flour to form dough that comes away from sides of bowl.
4. Turn out dough onto lightly floured surface. Knead for 10 to 12 minutes, adding enough flour to make dough smooth and elastic. Flatten on floured board to height of about 1 inch (2.5 cm). Sprinkle raisins on top and knead into dough. Place in greased bowl. Cover with greased waxed paper and tea towel. Let rise in warm place (75° to 85°F/24° to 29°C) until doubled, 1 to 1½ hours.
5. Punch down. Turn out onto lightly floured board and cut into two equal portions. Shape each into loaf. Place in prepared loaf pans. Cover with tea towel and let rise until doubled, about 1 hour. Bake for 15 minutes, then reduce oven temperature to 350°F (180°C) and bake for 35 to 45 minutes. Cover tops of bread with foil during last 15 minutes if becoming too brown. Remove from pan and cool on rack.

Preparation time: 30 minutes / Rising time: 2½ hours / Baking time: 1 hour / Freezing: excellent

Cheese Puffs

A fun-to-eat treat, these puffs are delicious served warm.

PREHEAT OVEN TO 375°F (190°C) • 10-INCH (4 L) TUBE PAN, GREASED

6½ cups	Robin Hood All-Purpose or Best For Bread Homestyle White Flour	1.625 L	**MAKES ABOUT 40 ROLLS**
1½ cups	shredded sharp Cheddar cheese	375 mL	
2½ tsp	salt	12 mL	**TIP:** Bread machine yeast works well, too.
2¼ tsp	quick-rise instant yeast (1 envelope ¼ oz/8 g)	11 mL	
1 tsp	granulated sugar	5 mL	
1½ cups	milk	375 mL	
½ cup	water	125 mL	
3 tbsp	butter or margarine	45 mL	
	Melted butter		
1½ cups	grated Parmesan cheese	375 mL	

1. Set aside 1 cup (250 mL) of the flour. Combine remaining flour, Cheddar cheese, salt, yeast and sugar in large mixing bowl.

2. Heat milk, water and 3 tbsp (50 mL) butter until hot to touch (125° to 130°F/ 50° to 55°C). Stir hot liquid into yeast mixture. Knead dough for about 10 minutes, adding reserved flour as necessary to make smooth, elastic and no longer sticky. Cover and let rest for 10 minutes.

3. Cut dough into 40 pieces. Shape into balls. Dip in melted butter, then roll in Parmesan cheese. Arrange in two layers in prepared pan. Cover with tea towel. Let rise in warm place (75° to 85°F/24° to 29°C) until balls come almost to top of pan, about 1 hour.

4. Bake for 40 to 50 minutes or until crisp. Cover with foil for last 10 minutes, if necessary, to prevent overbrowning of crust. Cool for 5 minutes, then remove from pan. Pull apart individual balls or slice.

Preparation time: 25 minutes / Rising time: 1 hour 10 minutes / Baking time: 50 minutes / Freezing: excellent

Make-Ahead Sticky Buns

Prepare the day before and enjoy fresh from the oven the next morning.

PREHEAT OVEN TO 350°F (180°C)
13- BY 9-INCH (3.5 L) CAKE PAN, GREASED

Dough

3½ to 4 cups	Robin Hood Best For Bread Homestyle White Flour	875 mL to 1 L
⅓ cup	granulated sugar	75 mL
1 tsp	salt	5 mL
4½ tsp	quick-rise instant yeast (2 envelopes ¼ oz/8 g each)	22 mL
1 cup	warm milk (100° to 110°F/38° to 45°C)	250 mL
⅓ cup	butter or margarine	75 mL
1	egg	1

Topping

1 cup	packed brown sugar	250 mL
½ cup	butter or margarine	125 mL
¼ cup	corn syrup	50 mL
1 cup	pecan halves	250 mL

Filling

2 tbsp	butter or margarine, softened	30 mL
¾ cup	chopped pecans	175 mL
¼ cup	packed brown sugar	50 mL
1½ tsp	cinnamon	7 mL

MAKES 15 BUNS

TIP: Use dark brown sugar for a more caramel taste.

1. Dough: Combine 2 cups (500 mL) of the flour, sugar, salt and yeast in large bowl. Add milk, butter and egg. Beat for 1 minute. Stir in enough of the remaining flour to make soft dough. Knead dough on floured board for 5 minutes. Place in greased bowl. Cover with plastic wrap. Let rise in warm place (75° to 85°F/24° to 29°C) until doubled, about 1¼ hours.

2. Topping: Bring brown sugar and butter to a boil. Stir in corn syrup. Pour into prepared pan. Sprinkle pecan halves on top.

3. Filling: Punch down dough. Roll out into 15- by 10-inch (37 x 25 cm) rectangle. Spread with butter. Combine pecans, brown sugar and cinnamon. Sprinkle over dough. Starting at long side, roll up tightly, pinching seam to seal. Cut into 15 pieces. Place in pan. Cover tightly with plastic wrap. Let rise in warm place for 1½ hours or in refrigerator for 12 to 48 hours or until doubled. Bake, uncovered, for 25 to 30 minutes or until golden. Let stand for 3 minutes in pan, then invert onto serving platter.

Preparation time: 25 minutes / Rising time: first 1¼ hours, second 1½ hours, or 12 to 48 hours / Baking time: 30 minutes / Freezing: excellent

Apricot Cheese Coffee Cake

An easy twisted dough top rises and puffs during baking to a very attractive finish.

PREHEAT OVEN TO 375°F (190°C)
9½-INCH (24 CM) SPRINGFORM PAN, SIDE RING REMOVED

Sweet Dough

¾ cup	warm milk	175 mL
1	egg, beaten	1
2 tbsp	butter	30 mL
2 cups	Robin Hood Best For Bread Homestyle White Flour	500 mL
¼ cup	granulated sugar	50 mL
¾ tsp	salt	3 mL
2 tsp	grated orange zest	10 mL
1½ tsp	bread machine yeast	7 mL

Filling

4 oz	spreadable cream cheese	125 g
1½ tbsp	Robin Hood Best For Bread Homestyle White Flour	22 mL
⅓ cup	apricot jam	75 mL
1	egg, beaten	1
2 tbsp	sliced almonds	30 mL

MAKES ABOUT 10 SERVINGS

TIP: Cool bread for about 30 minutes to let filling set before slicing.

1. Sweet Dough: Add all ingredients to bread machine according to manufacturer's directions. Select Dough cycle. Remove dough from pan. Cover and let rest for 10 minutes.

2. Filling: Roll out dough on lightly floured surface into 15-inch (37 cm) circle. Place dough on pan bottom. Combine cream cheese and flour. Spread cheese mixture in center of dough, covering area over top of pan. Spread jam over cheese. Make cuts about 1 inch (2.5 cm) apart around dough to about 1 inch (2.5 cm) away from filling. Twist pairs of dough strips together. Bring up to center covering filling. Place greased ring on pan bottom. Cover with tea towel. Let rise in warm place for 50 to 60 minutes or until almost doubled. Brush lightly with beaten egg. Sprinkle almonds on top. Bake for 30 to 35 minutes or until golden. Cover with foil after 20 minutes if becoming too brown.

VARIATION: Try other jams.

**Preparation time: 25 minutes / Rising time: approximately 3 hours /
Baking time: 35 minutes / Freezing: excellent**

Raisin Scones

Two different textures can be obtained in a matter of minutes!

PREHEAT OVEN TO 425°F (220°C) • BAKING SHEET, UNGREASED

2 cups	Robin Hood All-Purpose Flour or 2¼ cups (550 mL) Robin Hood Best For Cake & Pastry Flour	500 mL	MAKES 8 SERVINGS
¼ cup	granulated sugar	50 mL	
2½ tsp	baking powder	12 mL	
½ tsp	baking soda	2 mL	
½ tsp	salt	2 mL	
¼ cup	shortening	50 mL	
¾ cup	raisins	175 mL	
1 cup	buttermilk or soured milk	250 mL	

TIP: Brush top with beaten egg and sprinkle with sugar for an appealing golden color.

1. Combine flour, sugar, baking powder, baking soda and salt in mixing bowl. Cut in shortening with pastry blender until mixture resembles coarse crumbs. Add raisins and buttermilk, stirring with fork until all ingredients are moistened. (Dough should be sticky.)

2. Turn out dough onto well-floured surface and knead for 1 minute. Shape dough into ball. Pat down onto baking sheet to form circle ¾ inch (2 cm) thick and about 8 inches (20 cm) in diameter. Gently mark round into eight wedges with knife. Let rest for 10 minutes for scone-like texture or bake immediately for more cake-like texture. Bake for 20 to 25 minutes or until golden and set in center. Cover with foil if becoming too brown during baking. Serve warm.

VARIATION: Replace raisins with dried cranberries and add 1 tbsp (15 mL) grated orange zest to dry ingredients.

Preparation time: 15 minutes / Baking time: 25 minutes / Freezing: excellent

Zucchini Bread

A tasty recipe that's always popular. Moist and delicious, this loaf tastes great thinly sliced and buttered or spread with cream cheese.

PREHEAT OVEN TO 350°F (180°C)
TWO 8½- BY 4½-INCH (1.5 L) LOAF PANS, GREASED

1½ cups	Robin Hood All-Purpose Flour	375 mL
1½ cups	Robin Hood Whole Wheat Flour	375 mL
1 tsp	baking powder	5 mL
1 tsp	baking soda	5 mL
1 tsp	salt	5 mL
1½ tsp	cinnamon	7 mL
½ tsp	ground nutmeg	2 mL
3	eggs	3
1½ cups	granulated sugar	375 mL
1 cup	vegetable oil	250 mL
2 tsp	vanilla	10 mL
2 cups	shredded unpeeled zucchini	500 mL
½ cup	chopped walnuts	125 mL
½ cup	raisins	125 mL

MAKES 2 LOAVES

TIP: Use small zucchini. Large ones have tougher skins and a lot of seeds.

1. Combine first seven ingredients. Stir well to blend.
2. Beat eggs in large mixing bowl. Gradually beat in sugar, then oil and vanilla. Add dry ingredients gradually, mixing well. Stir in zucchini, walnuts and raisins. Pour batter into prepared pans. Bake for 55 to 60 minutes or until toothpick inserted in center comes out clean. Cool in pans for 10 minutes, then turn out onto rack to cool completely.

VARIATION: Replace zucchini with grated carrot.

Preparation time: 15 minutes / Baking time: 1 hour / Freezing: excellent

Glazed Lemon Nut Bread

Passed down from generation to generation, this wonderful loaf has passed the test of time.

PREHEAT OVEN TO 350°F (180°C) • 9- BY 5-INCH (2 L) LOAF PAN, GREASED

2 cups	Robin Hood All-Purpose Flour	500 mL
1 tsp	baking powder	5 mL
½ tsp	baking soda	2 mL
¼ tsp	salt	1 mL
1¼ cups	granulated sugar	300 mL
½ cup	shortening	125 mL
3	eggs	3
½ cup	lemon juice	125 mL
½ cup	milk	125 mL
¾ cup	chopped pecans	175 mL

Lemon Glaze

⅓ cup	confectioner's (icing) sugar, sifted	75 mL
¼ cup	lemon juice	50 mL

MAKES 1 LOAF

TIP: Try it toasted!

1. Stir together flour, baking powder, baking soda and salt. Set aside.
2. Beat sugar and shortening in large bowl on medium speed of electric mixer until fluffy. Add eggs, one at a time, beating well after each addition. Gradually beat in lemon juice. Add milk alternately with dry ingredients. Stir in nuts. Pour into prepared pan. Bake for 60 to 65 minutes or until toothpick inserted in center comes out clean. Remove from oven. While still in pan, poke holes with toothpick or fork in bread 1 inch (2.5 cm) apart.
3. Lemon Glaze: Stir together sugar and juice. Slowly pour half of the glaze over warm bread. Cool for 10 minutes. Remove from pan. Place on rack over piece of waxed paper. Pour remaining glaze over bread. Cool completely.

Preparation time: 15 minutes / Baking time: 1 hour 5 minutes / Freezing: excellent

Sesame Crisp Bread

A unique homemade cracker to serve with a dill dip or pâté at your next party.

PREHEAT OVEN TO 425°F (220°C) • BAKING SHEET, UNGREASED

1½ cups	Robin Hood All-Purpose Flour	375 mL
1 cup	Robin Hood Whole Wheat Flour	250 mL
½ tsp	salt	2 mL
1 cup	warm water	250 mL
1	egg, beaten	1
	Sesame seeds	
	Garlic powder	
	Finely chopped fresh dill or dried dillweed	

MAKES FOUR
12-INCH (30 CM)
ROUND FLAT BREADS

TIP: Black sesame seeds add interest.

1. Combine flours and salt in mixing bowl. Stir well to blend.
2. Add water to flour mixture. Stir with wooden spoon until mixture forms soft dough. Turn out dough onto floured surface and knead well for about 10 minutes or until smooth. Place in greased bowl; cover with damp cloth and allow to rest at room temperature for 2 hours.
3. Divide dough into four equal portions. Roll each piece into very thin round, approximately 12 inches (30 cm) in diameter. (Don't worry about an uneven shape. It's more interesting if circle isn't perfectly round.)
4. Transfer to baking sheet and brush lightly with beaten egg. Sprinkle lightly with sesame seeds, garlic powder and dill or other desired seasonings. Prick dough well with fork. Bake for 10 to 15 minutes or until crisp and lightly browned. Serve whole and break off pieces for eating.

VARIATION: Try different seasoning variations such as dried pepper flakes, sautéed onion and bacon, poppy seeds, finely chopped onion, grated Parmesan cheese and seasoning salt.

**Preparation time: 15 minutes / Resting time: 2 hours /
Baking time: 15 minutes / Freezing: excellent**

Pineapple Banana Loaf

A moist, tender banana loaf with bits of crushed pineapple throughout.
Enjoy one now and freeze one loaf for unexpected company.

PREHEAT OVEN TO 350°F (180°C)
TWO 8½- BY 4½-INCH (1.5 L) OR 9- BY 5-INCH (2 L) LOAF PANS, GREASED

3 cups	Robin Hood All-Purpose Flour	750 mL
2 cups	granulated sugar	500 mL
1 tsp	baking powder	5 mL
1 tsp	baking soda	5 mL
1 tsp	salt	5 mL
1 cup	crushed pineapple, undrained	250 mL
3	eggs	3
1¼ cups	vegetable oil	300 mL
2 cups	mashed ripe banana (about 5 bananas)	500 mL
2 tsp	vanilla	10 mL

MAKES 2 LOAVES

TIP: Brands of pineapple vary. Choose coarsely chopped fruit with a high proportion of fruit to juice.

1. Combine first five ingredients.
2. Beat together remaining ingredients in large bowl until blended. Add dry ingredients, stirring until thoroughly combined. Divide evenly between prepared pans. Bake for 60 to 70 minutes or until toothpick inserted in center comes out clean. Cool for 15 minutes in pan, then transfer to rack and cool completely.

VARIATION: Stir 1 cup (250 mL) chopped nuts into batter, if desired. Macadamia or Brazil nuts are nice.

Preparation time: 15 minutes / Baking time: 1 hour 10 minutes / Freezing: excellent

Nutty Seed Bread

A wonderful flavored loaf with lots of crunchy seeds. Try it toasted with honey.

PREHEAT OVEN TO 350°F (180°C) • 9- BY 5-INCH (2 L) LOAF PAN, GREASED

1	egg	1	MAKES 1 LOAF
1 cup	buttermilk or soured milk	250 mL	
⅓ cup	vegetable oil	75 mL	**TIP:** Store whole wheat flour well wrapped in the freezer to retain its freshness.
1 cup	Robin Hood All-Purpose Flour	250 mL	
1 cup	Robin Hood Whole Wheat Flour	250 mL	
1 cup	packed brown sugar	250 mL	
⅓ cup	finely chopped nuts	75 mL	
2 tbsp	each wheat germ, flaxseeds, sesame seeds, sunflower seeds and poppy seeds	30 mL	
1 tsp	baking powder	5 mL	
1 tsp	baking soda	5 mL	
½ tsp	salt	2 mL	

1. Combine first three ingredients in large mixing bowl.
2. Mix together remaining ingredients. Add to liquid ingredients, mixing to moisten all ingredients. Spread in prepared pan. Bake for 50 to 60 minutes or until toothpick inserted in center comes out clean. Cool for 10 minutes in pan, then remove and cool completely on rack.

VARIATION: Vary the type of nuts and seeds to suit your personal taste.

Preparation time: 15 minutes / Baking time: 1 hour / Freezing: excellent

Muffins

Banana Bran Muffins

Good-for-you bran muffins with a great banana taste.

PREHEAT OVEN TO 400°F (200°C) • 12-CUP MUFFIN PAN, GREASED

1½ cups	natural wheat bran	375 mL	
1 cup	Robin Hood All-Purpose Flour	250 mL	
½ cup	packed brown sugar	125 mL	
1½ tsp	baking powder	7 mL	
½ tsp	baking soda	2 mL	
¼ tsp	salt	1 mL	
1 tsp	cinnamon	5 mL	
½ cup	chopped walnuts, optional	125 mL	
2	eggs	2	
1 cup	mashed ripe bananas (2 to 3 bananas)	250 mL	
½ cup	milk	125 mL	
½ cup	butter or margarine, melted	125 mL	

MAKES 1 DOZEN MUFFINS

TIP: Use ripe bananas for the best flavor.

1. Combine first seven ingredients in large bowl. Stir in nuts.
2. Beat together remaining ingredients in small bowl. Add to dry ingredients, stirring just until combined. Spoon batter into prepared muffin pan. Bake for 18 to 20 minutes or until top springs back when lightly touched.

VARIATION: Omit cinnamon for a stronger banana taste.

Preparation time: 15 minutes / Baking time: 20 minutes / Freezing: excellent

Orange Date Oatmeal Muffins

Using a whole orange means a tangy muffin that's quick and easy to bake.

PREHEAT OVEN TO 400°F (200°C) • 12-CUP MUFFIN PAN, GREASED

1¼ cups	milk	300 mL
1 cup	Robin Hood or Old Mill Oats	250 mL
1	medium orange, seeded	1
1	egg	1
¾ cup	packed brown sugar	175 mL
½ cup	butter or margarine, melted	125 mL
½ cup	chopped dates	125 mL
2 cups	Robin Hood All-Purpose Flour	500 mL
1 tbsp	baking powder	15 mL
½ tsp	salt	2 mL

MAKES 1 DOZEN MUFFINS

TIP: Store muffins in airtight container to retain freshness.

1. Pour milk over oats in bowl. Let stand for 5 minutes.
2. Cut orange into quarters. Process in food processor or blender until finely chopped. Stir into oat mixture with egg, brown sugar, melted butter and dates.
3. Combine remaining ingredients in large bowl. Stir oat mixture into dry ingredients just until moistened. Spoon batter into prepared muffin pan, filling to top. Bake for 20 to 25 minutes or until top springs back when lightly touched.

VARIATION: Replace dates with raisins.

Preparation time: 15 minutes / Baking time: 25 minutes / Freezing: excellent

Peach Shortcake Muffins

Serve as a morning muffin or warm with whipped cream as a dessert.

PREHEAT OVEN TO 400°F (200°C) • 12-CUP MUFFIN PAN, GREASED

Muffin

1²⁄₃ cups	Robin Hood All-Purpose Flour	400 mL	
½ cup	granulated sugar	125 mL	
2½ tsp	baking powder	12 mL	
¼ tsp	salt	1 mL	
½ tsp	ground ginger	2 mL	
6 tbsp	butter or margarine	90 mL	
1 cup	milk	250 mL	
1²⁄₃ cups	coarsely chopped fresh or canned peaches	400 mL	

Topping

2 tbsp	granulated sugar	30 mL	
½ tsp	cinnamon	2 mL	

MAKES 1 DOZEN MUFFINS

TIP: To peel peaches easily, first dip in boiling water, then cold water.

1. Combine first five ingredients in large bowl. Cut in butter with pastry blender until crumbly. Add milk and peaches, stirring just until blended. Spoon batter into prepared muffin pan.

2. Topping: Combine sugar and cinnamon. Sprinkle over muffins. Bake for 20 to 25 minutes or until top springs back when lightly touched.

VARIATION: Replace peaches with fresh strawberries.

Preparation time: 20 minutes / Baking time: 25 minutes / Freezing: excellent

Cranberry Lemon Muffins

Tangy lemon and tart cranberries pair up for a refreshingly tasty muffin.

PREHEAT OVEN TO 400°F (200°C) • 12-CUP MUFFIN PAN, GREASED

2½ cups	Robin Hood All-Purpose Flour	625 mL	
1 tbsp	baking powder	15 mL	
½ tsp	salt	2 mL	
½ tsp	cinnamon	2 mL	
1	egg	1	
1¼ cups	milk	300 mL	
⅓ cup	vegetable oil	75 mL	
⅓ cup	liquid honey	75 mL	
2 tsp	grated lemon zest	10 mL	
1½ cups	fresh or frozen cranberries	375 mL	

Glaze (optional)

⅔ cup	confectioner's (icing) sugar, sifted	150 mL
1 tsp	grated lemon zest	5 mL
3 to 4 tsp	lemon juice	15 to 20 mL

MAKES 1 DOZEN MUFFINS

TIP: For a crunchy topping, sprinkle batter with a mixture of ⅓ cup (75 mL) chopped almonds and 2 tbsp (30 mL) granulated sugar before baking.

1. Combine first four ingredients.
2. Combine egg, milk, oil, honey and lemon zest in large bowl. Add dry ingredients. Stir just until dry ingredients are moistened. Fold in cranberries. Spoon batter into prepared muffin pan. Bake for 20 to 25 minutes or until top springs back when lightly touched.
3. Glaze: Combine confectioner's sugar, lemon zest and enough juice to make smooth, spreadable consistency. Spread on warm muffins.

VARIATION: Replace lemon zest and juice with orange.

Preparation time: 20 minutes / Baking time: 25 minutes / Freezing: excellent, not glazed

Cranberry Breakfast Muffins

Red River Cereal and oats combine with fresh cranberries in this hearty, healthy muffin.

PREHEAT OVEN TO 375°F (190°C) • 12-CUP MUFFIN PAN, GREASED

¾ cup	Robin Hood or Old Mill Oats	175 mL
½ cup	Red River Cereal	125 mL
1 cup	buttermilk or soured milk	250 mL
1 cup	Robin Hood All-Purpose Flour	250 mL
¾ cup	packed brown sugar	175 mL
1 tsp	baking powder	5 mL
¾ tsp	baking soda	3 mL
½ tsp	salt	2 mL
1	egg	1
⅓ cup	butter, melted	75 mL
1 cup	fresh or frozen cranberries	250 mL

MAKES 1 DOZEN MUFFINS

TIP: Keep a few bags of cranberries in your freezer to enjoy these muffins year-round.

1. Combine oats, Red River Cereal and buttermilk in large bowl. Let stand for 40 minutes. Combine flour, sugar, baking powder, baking soda and salt. Add egg and melted butter to cereal mixture. Add dry ingredients. Mix well. Stir in cranberries. Spoon batter into prepared muffin pan. Bake for 20 to 25 minutes or until top springs back when lightly touched.

VARIATION: Replace cranberries with blueberries.

Preparation time: 15 minutes / Standing time: 40 minutes / Baking time: 25 minutes / Freezing: excellent

Cranberry Banana Oat Muffins

Sweet bananas and tart cranberries combine for a great taste sensation.

PREHEAT OVEN TO 375°F (190°C) • 12-CUP MUFFIN PAN, GREASED

1¼ cups	Robin Hood All-Purpose Flour	300 mL
1 cup	Robin Hood or Old Mill Oats	250 mL
⅔ cup	granulated sugar	150 mL
1½ tsp	baking powder	7 mL
1 tsp	baking soda	5 mL
½ tsp	salt	2 mL
1	egg	1
1¾ cups	mashed ripe bananas (5 or 6 bananas)	425 mL
⅓ cup	butter or margarine, melted	75 mL
1 cup	cranberries	250 mL

MAKES 1 DOZEN MUFFINS

TIP: For an attractive finish, sprinkle some oats on top of muffins before baking.

1. Combine first six ingredients in mixing bowl. Mix well.
2. Beat together egg, bananas and melted butter until smooth. Add to dry ingredients. Stir to blend. Stir in cranberries just until combined. Spoon batter into prepared muffin pan, filling almost to top. Bake for 20 to 25 minutes or until top springs back when lightly touched.

VARIATION: For a heartier muffin, use Robin Hood Whole Wheat Flour.

Preparation time: 15 minutes / Baking time: 25 minutes / Freezing: excellent

Apple Cranberry Crumble Muffins

A crumbly almond streusel tops these huge, moist muffins.

PREHEAT OVEN TO 375°F (190°C) • 12-CUP MUFFIN PAN, GREASED

2¼ cups	Robin Hood All-Purpose Flour	550 mL
1¼ cups	packed brown sugar	300 mL
1 tsp	baking soda	5 mL
½ tsp	salt	2 mL
1	egg	1
1 cup	plain yogurt	250 mL
½ cup	vegetable oil	125 mL
2 cups	diced peeled apples	500 mL
¾ cup	cranberries	175 mL

Topping

¼ cup	packed brown sugar	50 mL
¼ cup	chopped almonds	50 mL
3 tbsp	Robin Hood or Old Mill Oats	45 mL
½ tsp	cinnamon	2 mL
1 tbsp	butter or margarine, melted	15 mL

MAKES 1 DOZEN MUFFINS

TIPS: Lightly toasting nuts before using brings out their flavor.

Grease top of pan as well as cups for easy removal.

1. Combine flour, brown sugar, baking soda and salt in large bowl.
2. Combine egg, yogurt and oil in small bowl. Add to dry ingredients, stirring just until moistened. Stir in apples and cranberries. Spoon batter into prepared muffin pan. (Cups will be very full.)
3. Topping: Combine all ingredients. Mix well and sprinkle over muffins. Bake for 25 to 30 minutes or until top springs back when lightly touched.

VARIATIONS: Replace cranberries with blueberries. Replace almonds with pecans.

Preparation time: 20 minutes / Baking time: 30 minutes / Freezing: excellent

Apple Bran Muffins

A very moist bran muffin with chunks of apple, raisins and a mild molasses taste.

PREHEAT OVEN TO 400°F (200°C) • 12-CUP MUFFIN PAN, GREASED

1 cup	packed brown sugar	250 mL
1	egg	1
1 cup	buttermilk or soured milk	250 mL
6 tbsp	butter or margarine, melted	90 mL
3 tbsp	molasses	45 mL
1½ cups	natural wheat bran	375 mL
1 cup	Robin Hood All-Purpose Flour	250 mL
1 tsp	baking soda	5 mL
½ tsp	baking powder	2 mL
½ tsp	salt	2 mL
1 cup	finely chopped peeled apple	250 mL
¾ cup	raisins	175 mL

MAKES 1 DOZEN MUFFINS

TIP: Natural wheat bran is small, dry and flaky; do not use the harder cereal pieces.

1. Combine first five ingredients in large mixing bowl. Mix well.
2. Combine bran, flour, baking soda, baking powder and salt. Stir into buttermilk mixture. Mix well. Stir in apple and raisins. Spoon batter into prepared muffin pan. Bake for 17 to 23 minutes or until top springs back when lightly touched.

VARIATION: Replace raisins with chopped dates.

Preparation time: 15 minutes / Baking time: 23 minutes / Freezing: excellent

Blueberry Oat Muffins

Try cranberries, raisins or chocolate chips for another muffin treat.

PREHEAT OVEN TO 375°F (190°C) • 12-CUP MUFFIN PAN, GREASED

1 cup	Robin Hood or Old Mill Oats	250 mL
1 cup	buttermilk or soured milk	250 mL
1 cup	Robin Hood All-Purpose Flour	250 mL
1 tsp	baking powder	5 mL
½ tsp	baking soda	2 mL
½ tsp	salt	2 mL
¾ cup	packed brown sugar	175 mL
1	egg	1
¼ cup	butter or margarine, melted	50 mL
1 cup	blueberries	250 mL

MAKES ABOUT
1 DOZEN MUFFINS

TIP: If wild blueberries are available, choose them for a wonderful flavor.

1. Combine oats and buttermilk. Let stand for 10 minutes.
2. Combine next five ingredients in large mixing bowl. Stir well to blend. Add egg and melted butter to oat mixture. Mix well. Add to dry ingredients, stirring just until moistened. Gently fold in blueberries. Spoon batter into prepared muffin pan. Bake for 20 to 25 minutes or until top springs back when lightly touched.

Preparation time: 15 minutes / Baking time: 25 minutes / Freezing: excellent

Strawberry Rhubarb Muffins

The top half is amazing, and the bottom is just as good.

PREHEAT OVEN TO 350°F (180°C) • TWO 12-CUP MUFFIN PANS, GREASED

2¾ cups	Robin Hood All-Purpose Flour	675 mL	
1¼ cups	packed brown sugar	300 mL	
1¼ tsp	baking soda	6 mL	
½ tsp	salt	2 mL	
½ cup	butter or margarine, melted	125 mL	
1	egg	1	
1 cup	buttermilk or soured milk	250 mL	
1¼ cups	chopped rhubarb	300 mL	
¾ cup	chopped strawberries	175 mL	

Topping

½ cup	packed brown sugar	125 mL	
½ tsp	cinnamon	2 mL	

MAKES 18 MUFFINS

TIP: Reheat previously frozen baked muffins in oven to crisp tops.

1. Combine first four ingredients. Mix well.
2. Combine melted butter, egg, buttermilk, rhubarb and strawberries in large mixing bowl. Add dry ingredients. Mix thoroughly until dry ingredients are moistened. Spoon batter into prepared muffin pans.
3. Topping: Combine brown sugar and cinnamon. Sprinkle evenly on muffins. Bake for 25 to 30 minutes or until top springs back when lightly touched.

VARIATION: Replace strawberries with raspberries or additional rhubarb.

Preparation time: 20 minutes / Baking time: 30 minutes / Freezing: excellent

Cocoa Oatmeal Muffins

Add cocoa powder to oatmeal muffins for a taste that's worth waking up to.
A creamy honey spread adds the crowning touch.

PREHEAT OVEN TO 400°F (200°C) • 12-CUP MUFFIN PAN, GREASED

1¼ cups	Robin Hood All-Purpose Flour	300 mL	
1 cup	granulated sugar	250 mL	
¾ cup	Robin Hood or Old Mill Oats	175 mL	
⅓ cup	cocoa powder	75 mL	
1 tbsp	baking powder	15 mL	
1 tsp	salt	5 mL	
2	eggs	2	
1 cup	milk	250 mL	
½ cup	butter or margarine, melted	125 mL	
1 tsp	vanilla	5 mL	
1 cup	chopped walnuts	250 mL	

Honey Spread

½ cup	butter or margarine, softened	125 mL
⅓ cup	liquid honey	75 mL

MAKES 1 DOZEN MUFFINS

TIPS: Sprinkle top of muffin batter with oats before baking, if desired.

Add chocolate chips for a more chocolatey taste.

1. Combine first six ingredients in large bowl. Mix well.
2. Beat together eggs, milk, melted butter and vanilla in small bowl. Add milk mixture and nuts all at once to dry ingredients, stirring just until moistened. Spoon batter into prepared muffin pan. Bake for 15 to 20 minutes or until top springs back when lightly touched.
3. Honey Spread: Beat together butter and honey until smooth. Spread on warm muffins.

Preparation time: 15 minutes / Baking time: 20 minutes / Freezing: excellent

Oat and Honey Bran Muffins

A tasty way to add nutrition to your diet!

PREHEAT OVEN TO 375°F (190°C) • TWO 12-CUP MUFFIN PANS, GREASED

1 cup	Robin Hood or Old Mill Oats	250 mL	
¾ cup	wheat germ	175 mL	
½ cup	natural wheat bran	125 mL	
½ tsp	salt	2 mL	
½ tsp	cinnamon	2 mL	
1 cup	buttermilk or soured milk	250 mL	
¾ cup	liquid honey	175 mL	
2	eggs, beaten	2	
½ cup	vegetable oil	125 mL	
1 cup	Robin Hood Whole Wheat Flour or All-Purpose Flour	250 mL	
2 tsp	baking powder	10 mL	
1 tsp	baking soda	5 mL	
½ cup	raisins	125 mL	

MAKES 18 MUFFINS

TIP: If you don't have buttermilk, pour 1 tbsp (15 mL) lemon juice in measuring cup. Add milk to make 1 cup (250 mL). Let stand for 5 minutes; stir.

1. Combine oats, wheat germ, bran, salt, cinnamon and buttermilk. Mix well and let stand for 15 minutes. Add honey, eggs and oil. Mix well.

2. Combine flour, baking powder and baking soda. Add to oat mixture. Stir just until moistened. Stir in raisins. Spoon batter into prepared muffin pans, filling three-quarters full. Bake for 20 to 25 minutes or until top springs back when lightly touched. Loosen edges and turn out onto racks to cool.

VARIATION: Dried cranberries or chopped apricots are also great.

Preparation time: 15 minutes / Baking time: 25 minutes / Freezing: excellent

Morning Muffin Magic

A nutritious and delicious way to start your day.

PREHEAT OVEN TO 350°F (180°C) • TWO 12-CUP MUFFIN PANS, GREASED

2 cups	Robin Hood All-Purpose Flour	500 mL
1¼ cups	granulated sugar	300 mL
2 tsp	baking soda	10 mL
2 tsp	cinnamon	10 mL
½ tsp	salt	2 mL
½ cup	raisins	125 mL
½ cup	chopped nuts	125 mL
½ cup	flaked coconut	125 mL
3	eggs	3
¾ cup	vegetable oil	175 mL
1 tsp	vanilla	7 mL
2 cups	grated peeled carrots	500 mL
1	grated peeled apple	1

MAKES 12 LARGE OR 16 REGULAR MUFFINS

TIPS: Be sure to peel the carrots. The reaction of peel in the batter can form green specks.

For large muffins, grease top of pan as well as cups. Cut overflowed tops in squares.

1. Combine first eight ingredients in large bowl. Stir well to blend.

2. Beat together eggs, oil, vanilla, carrots and apple in medium bowl. Add to dry ingredients, stirring just until moistened. Spoon batter into prepared muffin pans, filling three-quarters full for regular size or full for large size. Bake for 20 to 27 minutes or until top springs back when lightly touched.

VARIATION: Replace carrot with zucchini.

Preparation time: 15 minutes / Baking time: 27 minutes / Freezing: excellent

Holiday Baking

Fruit and Nut Refrigerator Cookies

A colorful cookie to have in your refrigerator — ready to just slice, bake and serve.

PREHEAT OVEN TO 375°F (190°C) • COOKIE SHEET, UNGREASED

2½ cups	Robin Hood All-Purpose Flour	625 mL
1 tsp	baking powder	5 mL
½ tsp	baking soda	2 mL
¼ tsp	salt	1 mL
½ cup	butter or margarine, softened	125 mL
½ cup	shortening	125 mL
1 cup	granulated sugar	250 mL
2	eggs	2
1 tsp	vanilla	5 mL
1 cup	chopped candied cherries or fruit	250 mL
½ cup	chopped nuts	125 mL

MAKES ABOUT
8 DOZEN COOKIES

TIP: Place cookies
2 inches (5 cm) apart
on baking sheet to
allow for spreading.

1. Combine flour, baking powder, baking soda and salt. Stir well to blend.

2. Cream butter, shortening, sugar, eggs and vanilla thoroughly. Stir flour mixture into creamed mixture. Mix well. Add fruit and nuts. If desired, refrigerate for 30 minutes for easier handling.

3. Shape dough into two smooth rolls about 1½ inches (4 cm) in diameter. Wrap in waxed paper and refrigerate until firm, about 4 hours or overnight. Slice with sharp knife into ¼-inch (5 mm) slices. Place on cookie sheet. Bake for 8 to 12 minutes or until golden. Cool for 5 minutes on sheet, then transfer to rack and cool completely.

Preparation time: 20 minutes / Refrigeration time: 4 hours or overnight / Baking time: 12 minutes / Freezing: excellent

Swedish Butter Balls

A melt-in-your-mouth delight that's loaded with nuts.

PREHEAT OVEN TO 400°F (200°C) • COOKIE SHEET, UNGREASED

1 cup	butter, softened	250 mL
½ cup	confectioner's (icing) sugar, sifted	125 mL
1 tsp	vanilla	5 mL
2½ cups	Robin Hood Best For Cake & Pastry Flour or 2¼ cups (550 mL) Robin Hood All-Purpose Flour	625 mL
1 cup	finely chopped pecans	250 mL
	Confectioner's (icing) sugar, sifted	

MAKES ABOUT
4½ DOZEN COOKIES

TIP: Work dough with your hands to get it smooth.

1. Cream butter, confectioner's sugar and vanilla thoroughly. Add flour. Mix well. Stir in nuts, mixing until smooth.

2. Shape dough into 1-inch (2.5 cm) balls. Place on cookie sheet. Bake for 8 to 12 minutes or until very light golden. Cool for 5 minutes on sheet, then transfer to rack and cool completely. Roll in confectioner's sugar.

VARIATION: Try hazelnuts or almonds.

Preparation time: 20 minutes / Baking time: 12 minutes / Freezing: excellent

Place Card Sugar Cookies

An old-fashioned melt-in-your-mouth cookie that's great for the holiday season.

PREHEAT OVEN TO 375°F (190°C) • COOKIE SHEET, GREASED • COOKIE CUTTERS

3 cups	Robin Hood All-Purpose Flour	750 mL	**MAKES ABOUT 4 DOZEN COOKIES**
1 tsp	baking powder	5 mL	
½ tsp	salt	2 mL	**TIP:** Cookies can be prepared ahead and decorated as needed.
1 cup	butter, softened	250 mL	
1¼ cups	granulated sugar	300 mL	
3	eggs	3	
1 tsp	vanilla	5 mL	
	Colored sugar, nuts, candies colored icings		

1. Combine flour, baking powder and salt. Stir well to blend. Cream butter and sugar with electric mixer until light and fluffy. Beat in eggs and vanilla. Stir flour mixture into creamed mixture. Mix well.

2. Form dough into two balls. Wrap in plastic wrap and refrigerate for about 3 hours. Roll out dough on floured surface to ¼-inch (5 mm) thickness. Cut into desired shapes. Place on prepared cookie sheet. (If cookies are to be used as Christmas tree ornaments or as gift tags, insert toothpick through end of cookie and leave during baking.)

3. Decorate with colored sugar, nuts or candies before baking or leave plain and decorate with icing later. Bake for 8 to 10 minutes or until light golden. Remove toothpicks. Cool for 5 minutes on sheet, then transfer to rack and cool completely. When cool, decorate with colored icings, if desired. Personalize cookies with a name written in icing. Thread with colorful ribbon, yarn or cord.

Preparation time: 20 minutes / Baking time: 10 minutes / Refrigeration time: 3 hours / Freezing: excellent

Empire Cookies

A long-time favorite cookie that's pretty at Christmas.

PREHEAT OVEN TO 350°F (180°C) • COOKIE SHEET, GREASED

Cookie

¾ cup	shortening	175 mL	
1 cup	granulated sugar	250 mL	
2	eggs	2	
1 tsp	vanilla	5 mL	
2¼ cups	Robin Hood All-Purpose Flour	550 mL	
1½ tsp	baking powder	7 mL	
¼ tsp	salt	1 mL	

Filling & Frosting

½ cup	raspberry jam	125 mL
1½ cups	confectioner's (icing) sugar, sifted	375 mL
¼ tsp	almond extract, optional	1 mL
1½ to 2 tbsp	hot water	22 to 30 mL
	Candied cherries	

MAKES ABOUT
3½ DOZEN COOKIES

TIP: A floured pastry cloth and rolling pin cover will make rolling out dough easy.

1. Cookie: Cream shortening, sugar, eggs and vanilla in large bowl on medium speed of electric mixer until light and creamy. Combine flour, baking powder and salt. Add to creamed mixture, beating at low speed until well blended. If desired, refrigerate for 1 hour for easy rolling. Roll out dough, one portion at a time, on lightly floured surface to ⅛-inch (3 mm) thickness. Cut into 2-inch (5 cm) rounds. Reroll leftover pieces. Place on prepared cookie sheet. Bake for 6 to 9 minutes or until lightly browned around edges. Cool for 5 minutes on sheet, then transfer to rack and cool completely.

2. Filling & Frosting: Spread underside of half of the cookies with jam. Top with remaining cookies to form sandwiches. Combine confectioner's sugar, almond extract and enough hot water to make a thin frosting. Frost tops of cookies. Decorate with small piece of cherry. Store in airtight container overnight.

Preparation time: 30 minutes / Baking time: 9 minutes / Freezing: excellent

Oatmeal Shortbread

Enjoy a unique texture and the flavor of oats in this melt-in-your mouth shortbread.

PREHEAT OVEN TO 300°F (150°C) • COOKIE SHEET, UNGREASED
COOKIE CUTTERS

¾ cup	Robin Hood All-Purpose Flour	175 mL	
⅔ cup	Robin Hood or Old Mill Oats	150 mL	
½ cup	cornstarch	125 mL	
½ cup	confectioner's (icing) sugar, sifted	125 mL	
¾ cup	butter, softened	175 mL	

MAKES ABOUT
2½ DOZEN COOKIES

TIP: Use quick oats, not instant.

1. Combine flour, oats, cornstarch and confectioner's sugar in large bowl. With large spoon, blend in butter. Work with hands until soft, smooth dough forms. Shape into ball. If necessary, refrigerate for 30 minutes or until easy to handle.

2. Roll out dough to ¼-inch (5 mm) thickness. Cut into shapes with cookie cutters. Place on cookie sheet. Decorate if desired. Bake for 15 to 25 minutes or until edges are lightly browned. (Time will depend on cookie size.) Cool for 5 minutes on sheet, then transfer to rack and cool completely. Store in tightly covered container.

VARIATION: Cranberry Wedges: Add ⅓ cup (75 mL) chopped dried cranberries to dough. Roll out or pat dough into two 5½-inch (14 cm) rounds about ½ inch (1 cm) thick on cookie sheet or press into one 9-inch (23 cm) cake pan. Mark into eight wedges. Prick with fork. Bake for 30 to 40 minutes for small rounds or for 40 to 45 minutes for larger round.

Preparation time: 20 minutes / Baking time: 25 minutes / Freezing: excellent

Hazelnut Shortbread Refrigerator Cookies

Prepare the rolls ahead so that they're ready to bake whenever you are.

PREHEAT OVEN TO 375°F (190°C) • COOKIE SHEET, UNGREASED

1 cup	Robin Hood All-Purpose Flour	250 mL	
½ cup	cornstarch	125 mL	
½ cup	confectioner's (icing) sugar, sifted	125 mL	
¾ cup	finely chopped hazelnuts	175 mL	
¾ cup	butter, softened	175 mL	

MAKES ABOUT 3 DOZEN COOKIES

TIP: Leave skins on hazelnuts.

1. Combine flour, cornstarch, confectioner's sugar and nuts in large bowl. With large spoon, blend in butter. Work with hands until soft, smooth dough forms.

2. Shape dough into smooth roll about 1½ inches (4 cm) in diameter. Wrap and refrigerate until firm, about 4 hours or overnight. Store rolls in refrigerator for up to 1 month.

3. Cut with sharp knife into thin slices. Place on cookie sheet. Bake for 8 to 12 minutes or until edges are lightly browned. Cool for 5 minutes on sheet, then transfer to rack and cool completely.

VARIATION: Cherry Pecan Shortbread: Omit hazelnuts. Mix dough until smooth, then mix in ¾ cup (175 mL) chopped candied cherries and ½ cup (125 mL) chopped pecans until evenly distributed.

Preparation time: 15 minutes / Refrigeration time: 4 hours or overnight / Baking time: 12 minutes / Freezing: excellent

Cherry Almond Macaroons

Moist, chewy and colorful; a new twist on an old favorite.

PREHEAT OVEN TO 350°F (180°C) • COOKIE SHEET, GREASED

4	eggs, separated	4	
¼ tsp	salt	1 mL	
1½ cups	granulated sugar	375 mL	
3 cups	flaked coconut	750 mL	
1½ cups	Robin Hood All-Purpose Flour or 1⅔ cups (400 mL) Robin Hood Best For Cake & Pastry Flour	375 mL	
1½ cups	chopped red or green candied cherries	375 mL	
1½ tsp	almond extract	7 mL	

MAKES ABOUT 45 COOKIES

TIP: Store soft cookies in airtight container with waxed paper between layers.

1. Beat egg whites and salt in small bowl on high speed of electric mixer until foamy. Gradually add sugar, beating until very stiff, about 4 minutes.
2. Beat egg yolks in large mixing bowl. Stir in coconut. Add flour, cherries and almond extract; mix well. Stir in egg white mixture thoroughly. (Mixture will be very stiff.)
3. Drop dough by tablespoonfuls (15 mL) about 2 inches (5 cm) apart onto prepared cookie sheet. Bake for 10 to 15 minutes or until set and edges are very light golden. Cool for 5 minutes on sheet, then transfer to rack and cool completely.

VARIATION: Substitute 1½ cups (375 mL) slivered almonds or a mixture of cherries and almonds for candied cherries.

Preparation time: 15 minutes / Baking time: 15 minutes / Freezing: excellent

Festive Fruitcake Cookies

Chock-full of fruit and nuts, these taste like mini fruitcakes.

PREHEAT OVEN TO 350°F (180°C) • COOKIE SHEET, GREASED

1 cup	raisins	250 mL
1 cup	candied cherries, coarsely chopped	250 mL
1 cup	candied pineapple, coarsely chopped	250 mL
1 cup	Brazil nuts, coarsely chopped	250 mL
½ cup	shortening	125 mL
¾ cup	granulated sugar	175 mL
1	egg	1
1 tsp	vanilla	5 mL
½ tsp	almond extract	2 mL
1¼ cups	Robin Hood All-Purpose Flour	300 mL
½ tsp	baking soda	2 mL
½ tsp	salt	2 mL

**MAKES ABOUT
3 DOZEN COOKIES**

TIP: Store cookies at room temperature for a day to let flavors mellow before eating.

1. Combine raisins, candied fruit and nuts. Mix well.
2. Cream shortening, sugar, egg, vanilla and almond extract in large bowl on medium speed of electric mixer until light and creamy.
3. Combine flour, baking soda and salt. Add to creamed mixture, beating on low speed until blended. Stir in fruit mixture. Mix well.
4. Drop dough by heaping tablespoonfuls (20 mL) about 2 inches (5 cm) apart onto prepared cookie sheet. Bake for 10 to 15 minutes or until golden. Cool for 5 minutes on sheet, then transfer to rack and cool completely.

VARIATION: Replace cherries and pineapple with mixed candied fruit.

Preparation time: 15 minutes / Baking time: 15 minutes / Freezing: excellent

Raspberry Pinwheel Refrigerator Cookies

Keep a roll handy in the refrigerator to bake whenever you need them.

PREHEAT OVEN TO 375°F (190°C) • COOKIE SHEET, GREASED

1¾ cups	Robin Hood All-Purpose Flour	425 mL
2 tsp	baking powder	10 mL
¼ tsp	salt	1 mL
½ cup	butter or margarine, softened	125 mL
1 cup	granulated sugar	250 mL
1	egg	1
1 tsp	vanilla	5 mL
½ cup	raspberry jam	125 mL
½ cup	flaked coconut	125 mL
⅓ cup	finely chopped pecans or walnuts	75 mL

MAKES ABOUT 3 DOZEN COOKIES

TIP: Rolls can be frozen. Thaw overnight in refrigerator before slicing.

1. Combine flour, baking powder and salt.
2. Cream butter, sugar, egg and vanilla thoroughly. Add dry ingredients, mixing well. Work with hands to form smooth dough. Roll out dough between two sheets of lightly floured waxed paper into 12- by 9-inch (30 by 23 cm) rectangle.
3. Combine jam, coconut and nuts. Spread evenly over dough, leaving ½-inch (1 cm) border. Roll up tightly, jelly roll fashion, using waxed paper to help, starting from long side. Press edge to seal and shape into roll. Wrap in plastic wrap. Refrigerate overnight.
4. Cut into ¼-inch (5 mm) thick slices. Place on prepared cookie sheet. Bake for 12 to 16 minutes or until golden. Cool for 5 minutes on sheet, then transfer to rack and cool completely.

VARIATION: Replace raspberry jam with apricot.

Preparation time: 25 minutes / Refrigeration time: overnight / Baking time: 16 minutes / Freezing: excellent

Chewy Cherry Bars

A colorful addition to your Christmas cookie tray.

PREHEAT OVEN TO 350°F (180°C) • 13- BY 9-INCH (3.5 L) CAKE PAN, GREASED

Crust

1 cup	Robin Hood All-Purpose Flour	250 mL	
1 cup	Robin Hood or Old Mill Oats	250 mL	
1 cup	packed brown sugar	250 mL	
1 tsp	baking soda	5 mL	
½ cup	butter	125 mL	

Filling

2	eggs	2	
1 cup	packed brown sugar	250 mL	
½ tsp	almond extract	2 mL	
2 tbsp	Robin Hood All-Purpose Flour	30 mL	
1 tsp	baking powder	5 mL	
¼ tsp	salt	1 mL	
1 cup	flaked coconut	250 mL	
1 cup	maraschino cherries, drained and coarsely chopped	250 mL	
½ cup	chopped pecans or walnuts	125 mL	

Frosting

¼ cup	butter, softened	50 mL	
½ tsp	almond extract	2 mL	
2 cups	confectioner's (icing) sugar, sifted	500 mL	
3 to 4 tbsp	milk or cream	45 to 60 mL	

MAKES ABOUT
4 DOZEN BARS

TIP: For bars with frosting, cut, place on foil tray and freeze to harden frosting. Then wrap in plastic bags to store in freezer. Remove individual bars as needed.

1. Crust: Combine flour, oats, brown sugar and baking soda in mixing bowl. Cut in butter until crumbly. Press into prepared pan. Bake for 10 minutes.

2. Filling: Beat together eggs, brown sugar and almond extract. Combine flour, baking powder and salt. Stir into egg mixture. Mix well. Stir in coconut, cherries and nuts. Spread evenly over crust. Bake for 25 minutes or until lightly browned. Cool completely.

3. Frosting: Beat together all ingredients until smooth and creamy. Spread over top. Chill until icing is firm, about 30 minutes. Cut into bars.

Preparation time: 20 minutes / Baking time: 35 minutes / Freezing: excellent

Fabulous Fruitcake

Prepare a few months in advance to let flavors mellow.

PREHEAT OVEN TO 275°F (140°C)
THREE 9- BY 5-INCH (2 L) LOAF PANS, GREASED, LINED WITH
ALUMINUM FOIL AND GREASED AGAIN

Fruits & Nuts

1 cup	chopped dried apricots	250 mL
3 cups	raisins	750 mL
2 cups	candied pineapple, coarsely chopped	500 mL
2 cups	candied cherries, halved	500 mL
2 cups	mixed candied peel	500 mL
2 cups	coarsely chopped pecans	500 mL
1 cup	slivered almonds	250 mL
1 cup	Robin Hood All-Purpose Flour	250 mL

Batter

1½ cups	Robin Hood All-Purpose Flour	375 mL
1 tsp	baking powder	5 mL
½ tsp	salt	2 mL
1 tsp	cinnamon	5 mL
½ tsp	ground nutmeg	2 mL
¼ tsp	ground cloves	1 mL
1¼ cups	butter, softened	300 mL
1½ cups	liquid honey	375 mL
1 tbsp	vanilla	15 mL
6	eggs	6

MAKES 3 LOAVES

TIP: Don't overbake. Cakes continue baking a little after removing from oven.

1. Fruits & Nuts: Combine all ingredients. Mix well to thoroughly coat fruits with flour.

2. Batter: Combine flour, baking powder, salt and spices. Mix well. Cream butter, honey and vanilla on medium speed of electric mixer. Add eggs, one at a time, beating well after each addition. Add dry ingredients on low speed, mixing just until blended. Stir in fruit and nut mixture. Mix well.

3. Spread batter evenly in prepared pans. Keeping pan of hot water in oven, bake for 2 to 2½ hours or until toothpick inserted in center comes out clean. Cool in pans. Remove foil. Wrap well and store in cool, dry place.

VARIATION: Vary the candied fruit and nuts to suit your own tastes. Keep the total amount the same as the recipe recommends.

Preparation time: 20 minutes / Baking time: 2 ½ hours / Freezing: excellent

Holiday Mincemeat Cake

Enjoy the moist, delicious flavor of mincemeat all year.

PREHEAT OVEN TO 350°F (180°C)
10-INCH (3 L) BUNDT PAN OR 13- BY 9-INCH (3.5 L) CAKE PAN,
GREASED AND FLOURED

3½ cups	Robin Hood All-Purpose Flour	875 mL	MAKES ABOUT 12 SERVINGS
3½ tsp	baking powder	17 mL	
1 tsp	baking soda	5 mL	
¾ tsp	salt	3 mL	**TIP:** Mincemeat not only keeps baked goods moist but adds a unique flavor as well.
¾ cup	butter, softened	175 mL	
4 tsp	grated orange zest	20 mL	
1½ tsp	vanilla	7 mL	
1 cup	granulated sugar	250 mL	
3	eggs	3	
3 cups	prepared mincemeat	750 mL	
¾ cup	milk	175 mL	
1 cup	chopped walnuts	250 mL	
	Confectioner's (icing) sugar		

1. Combine flour, baking powder, baking soda and salt. Set aside.
2. Cream butter, orange zest and vanilla in large bowl on medium speed of electric mixer until light. Beat in sugar. Add eggs, one at a time, beating well after each addition. Blend in mincemeat. Add dry ingredients to mincemeat mixture alternately with milk, beginning and ending with dry ingredients. Stir in nuts. Pour batter into prepared pan. Bake for 55 to 60 minutes for Bundt pan, 45 to 50 minutes for rectangular pan, or until toothpick inserted in center comes out clean. Cool in pan for 20 minutes. Remove from pan; cool completely. Dust with confectioner's sugar before serving.

Preparation time: 15 minutes / Baking time: 50 or 60 minutes / Freezing: excellent

Cherry Bundt Cake

A colorful cake for the Christmas season but enjoyable all year round.

PREHEAT OVEN TO 350°F (180°C)
10-INCH (3 L) BUNDT PAN OR 10-INCH (4 L) TUBE PAN, GREASED AND FLOURED

1¼ cups	butter, softened	300 mL
2¾ cups	granulated sugar	675 mL
5	eggs	5
1 tsp	almond extract	5 mL
3 cups	Robin Hood All-Purpose Flour	750 mL
1 tsp	baking powder	5 mL
¼ tsp	salt	1 mL
1 cup	undiluted evaporated milk	250 mL
2 cups	quartered maraschino cherries, well drained	500 mL
	Confectioner's (icing) sugar, optional	

MAKES ABOUT
16 SERVINGS

TIP: A white icing drizzle is a pretty alternative decoration.

1. Beat butter, sugar, eggs and almond extract in large bowl on low speed of electric mixer until blended, then on high speed for 5 minutes until light and fluffy. Combine flour, baking powder and salt. Add dry ingredients to butter mixture alternately with evaporated milk, mixing lightly after each addition. Fold in cherries. Pour batter into prepared pan.

2. Bake for 75 to 85 minutes or until toothpick inserted in center comes out clean. Cover with foil for first 10 minutes if becoming too brown. Cool in pan for 20 minutes. Remove from pan and cool completely. Dust with confectioner's sugar before serving, if desired.

VARIATION: Replace half the cherries with candied pineapple.

Preparation time: 20 minutes / Baking time: 1 hour 25 minutes / Freezing: excellent

Cranberry Orange Bubble Bread

Prepare the dough in a bread machine, then finish baking in a conventional oven.

PREHEAT OVEN TO 375°F (190°C) • 9-INCH (23 CM) SPRINGFORM PAN, GREASED
BREAD MACHINE

Dough

1 cup	milk, at room temperature	250 mL	MAKES ABOUT
1	egg	1	10 SERVINGS
1 tbsp	butter or margarine	15 mL	
3 cups	Robin Hood Best For Bread Homestyle White Flour	750 mL	**TIP:** For an attractive finish, drizzle with a white icing or sprinkle
1 tbsp	granulated sugar	15 mL	with confectioner's
2 tsp	grated orange zest	10 mL	sugar. Leftovers
1 tsp	salt	5 mL	make wonderful
¾ cup	dried cranberries	175 mL	bread pudding and
2 tsp	bread machine yeast	10 mL	French toast.

Glaze (optional)

1	egg, beaten	1

1. Dough: Add all ingredients to bread machine according to manufacturer's directions. Select Dough cycle.
2. Divide dough into 16 pieces. Shape each piece into ball. Place in prepared pan. Cover with tea towel. Let rise in warm place (75° to 85°F/24° to 29°C) until doubled, about 45 minutes.
3. Glaze: Brush lightly with beaten egg for a shiny, golden top.
4. Bake on lower oven rack for 20 to 25 minutes or until golden. Cover top with aluminum foil if becoming too brown. Remove from pan immediately. Cool on rack.

VARIATION: Replace cranberries with dried cherries, chopped apricots or raisins.

**Preparation time: 15 minutes / Rising time: 45 minutes /
Baking time: 25 minutes / Freezing: excellent**

Cranberry Chocolate Orange Rounds

Soup cans make ideal baking pans for round cranberry loaves. These make wonderful Christmas gifts.

PREHEAT OVEN TO 350°F (180°C) • TEN 10-OZ (284 ML) CANS, WELL GREASED

2 cups	fresh or frozen cranberries, coarsely chopped	500 mL	**MAKES 10 MINI LOAVES**
½ cup	granulated sugar	125 mL	
3½ cups	Robin Hood All-Purpose Flour	875 mL	**TIPS:** These make wonderful hostess gifts any time of the year.
1½ cups	granulated sugar	375 mL	
1 tbsp	baking powder	15 mL	
1 tsp	baking soda	5 mL	For two 9- by 5-inch (2 L) loaves, use 2 tsp (10 mL) baking powder and bake for 70 minutes.
1 tsp	salt	5 mL	
2	eggs	2	
1 tbsp	grated orange zest	15 mL	
1⅓ cups	orange juice	325 mL	
¼ cup	vegetable oil	50 mL	
2 cups	miniature semi-sweet chocolate chips	500 mL	
1 cup	chopped nuts, optional	250 mL	

1. Combine cranberries and ½ cup (125 mL) sugar. Set aside.
2. Combine flour, 1½ cups (375 mL) sugar, baking powder, baking soda and salt in mixing bowl. Stir well to blend.
3. Beat together eggs, orange zest, juice and oil. Add to dry ingredients, stirring just until moistened. Fold in cranberry mixture, chocolate chips, and nuts, if desired. Divide batter among prepared cans. Bake for 35 to 40 minutes or until toothpick inserted in center comes out clean. Cool for 10 minutes, then run thin-blade knife around sides of cans to loosen. Turn out onto rack to cool completely. Wrap and store overnight before slicing or freeze for later use.

Preparation time: 15 minutes / Baking time: 40 minutes / Freezing: excellent

Index